STILL THOUGHTS VOIUME TWO BY DHARMA MASTER CHENG YEN

Transtated by Liu King-Pong
English Edited by Sam Dixon

First published in February 1995
Still Thoughts Culture Publications, 35 Chung
Hsiao E. Rd., Sec 3, Lane 217, Alley 7, Taipei,
Taiwan. R.O.C.

Printed by U-Wen Printing Co., Ltd.
Publisher : Chen Yen
NT$:150
ISBN 957-99836-1-5

Preface

The Tang dynasty poet Liu Yu-hsi once wrote:

In the noisy Chutang Gorge, the river roars past six sand spits and six more. The path through the chasm's heart has been treacherous from the start. Often, I have deplored that our hearts are not more like the river's roar, which is still until it hits the gorge's dozen sandy spits.

In this poem, Liu Yu-hsi describes how water will only leave its normally tranquil state to become something awesome and terrifying when it abruptly meets a rock or other obstacle. The poet then portrays the hearts of men as more turbulent than the movement of water, contrasting the treacherous path through the Chutang Gorge with the spiritual journey of the heart which, he believes, is even more perilous. This poem on the heart's permutations is charged

3

with emotions that many of us can empathize with. Men's hearts, though so difficult to adjust, are yet adjustable. If we reflect inward and meditate on what we have done and what we will do, our hearts can become as still and transparent as a pool of quiet water. Since the publication of Still Thoughts, I have received much praise and encouragement from the public, for which I feel deeply grateful and humbled. I hope this present edition will bring levity and peace to your being, and a measure of understanding and realization. *Still Thoughts: Volume Two* is published and distributed by both the Chiu-Ko Publishing Co. and the Tzu-Chi Cultural and Publishing Co. Volume Two has the same format and style as its predecessor, but we have enlarged the scope of its contents to offer a broader range of thoughts for our readers. Zen masters throughout the ages have said, "The written word might obstruct an understanding of the Buddhist Way." This is why they seldom left written sutras for later generations, instead teaching us to think for ourselves. Indeed, the Buddhist Way lies not in the written word or in language but in the heart itself. We will never understand the Buddhist Way if we get stuck in the written word and fail to read between the lines and act accordingly.

The relationship between the written word and the Buddhist Way is like "pointing at the moon with your finger." The aim is to look at the moon, not at your finger. The written word may indeed point to the meaning of the Buddhist Way, but it would be a mistake to neglect the object of study by overemphasizing the pointers we employ.

Thus, in *Still Thoughts* I have used simple words to explain the meaning of life, hoping that each reader will easily understand it and feel at ease within himself. To some extent, the first volume has already had this effect.

Wang An-shih, a poet in the Sung dynasty, once wrote the following ditty describing how simple lyrics can actually contain much profound thought.

Famous bard was he, the Music Steward of Soochow. The music bureau staff agreed his lyrics unearthly glowed. What seemed common at the start were fancy in the end.

His lyrics were easily art but not so readily penned.

STILL THOUGHTS

Seldom are we able to appreciate the truth by reading florid writing. Common everyday expressions can reveal much more about the nature of Buddha, if you only think deeply about them.

"The presence of a single plum blossom can give a new cast to the light of the moon." *Still thought* entails thinking calmly and combining one's physical and spiritual strengths. By practicing still thought, you can be inspired by even a single phrase.

Still Thoughts: Volume Two will soon be published. I dare not believe that it will help purify some of our vulgar customs. But, I do hope it can, as a duty of mine, imperceptibly influence some people in our society. The realization of my hope depends on how much truth you obtain through reading a sentence or two in *Still Thoughts: Volume Two*.

Cheng Yen

October, 14, 1991

Pure Abode Compound, Hualien

Translated by Liu King-pong

6

Table of Contents

Preface————————————————————————3

Part 1: The Dawn of Still Thoughts

Chapter One:Allow Life to Function Always Like a Spring Day————————————————2
(The Coal of Life)

Chapter Two: The Starting Point of Success————————————————————————6
(Speaking of Perseverance)

Chapter Three: A Sweet Fountain in a Dessert————————————————————————8

STILL THOUGHTS

(The Spirit of Religion)

Chapter Four: The Personification of Mercy and Wisdom——————————————*11*
(The Heart of a Bodhisattva)

Chapter Five: We Came Nakedly Into the World——————————————*15*
(Making Good Use of Our Bodies)

Chapter Six: The River of Love Can Be as Dangerous as a Tidal Wave————————*18*
(Speaking of Love and Romance)

Chapter Seven: We Should Do More Than Simply Talk a Lot——————————*24*
(Speaking on the Cultivation of Morality)

Chapter Eight: The Proper Way to Manage Finances————————————————*38*

(Speaking About Money and Finance)

Chapter Nine: To Light a Lamp in the Dark

————————————————————————*42*

(Speaking About Imitating Buddha's Behavior)

Chapter Ten: Personal Growth in a Challenging World————————————————*50*

(Speaking About the Hardships of Life)

Chapter Eleven: Healthy Yet Useless————*56*

(Speaking About Wrongdoing)

Chapter Twelve: Many Grains of Rice Make a Bushel————————————————*58*

(Many a Little Makes a Mickle)

STILL THOUGHTS

Chapter Thirteen: Don't Choose a Venomous Snake as Your Companion———60
(The Five Poisons of Greed, Anger, Delusion, Arrogance and Suspicion)

Chapter Fourteen: Tolerance———66
(To Bear Disgrace and Insult)

Chapter Fifteen: Do Not Plant Poison Ivy in your Heart———70
(Speaking About Mentality)

Chapter Sixteen: A Sutra We Must Read
———79
(Talking About Family Ethics)

Chapter Seventeen: March to Life's Tune
———83

Table of Contents

(Speaking About Pure Love)

Chapter Eighteen: Great Teamwork————92
(Speaking About Service, Duty and Gratitude)

Chapter Nineteen: A Spiritual Antibody——96
(Speaking About Confidence, Perseverance and Courage)

Chapter Twenty: We Should Often Draw the Well Water————————————100
(Speaking About Luck, Fortune and Happiness)

Chapter Twenty—One: Spiritual Relief——105
(Speaking About Mercy and Wisdom)

Chapter Twenty—Two: To Sprinkle a Drop of Sweet Dew————————110

STILL THOUGHTS

(Less Desire and More Contentment)

Chapter Twenty—Three: Mastery Comes From Training————————————————*115*
(Speaking About the Ego—Center)

Chapter Twenty—Four: We Come and Go Empty—Handed————————————————*120*
(Speaking About Letting It Go)

Chapter Twenty—Five: The Enormous Power of Compassion————————————————*123*
(Speaking About the Spiritual Careers of the Tzu Chi Association)

Chapter Twenty—Six: Drinking the Water of the Glass of Wisdom————————————————*128*
(Speaking About Delivery, Impermanence and

Rapid Progress)

Chapter Twenty—Seven: Let Everyone Have a Smiling Face————————————*134*
(Abstaining From Slaughter)

Chapter Twenty—Eight: Life Is Short——*138*
(How to Live a Fruitful Life)

Chapter Twenty—nine: Our Hearts Are the Dwellings for Studying Buddhist Philosophy
————————————————*142*

(How to Get Along With Others and Deal With Problems)

Part 2: Questions & Answers

Section One: Human Affairs

STILL THOUGHTS

Speaking About Love—————————————146

Speaking About Daughter and Mother-in-law
————————————————————166

Speaking About Illness—————————170

Speaking About One's Mindset————177

Speaking About Life———————————188

Speaking About Tolerating Insults————191

Speaking About Mercy—————————194

Speaking About Daily Affairs——————199

Speaking About Learning————————211

Speaking About Time——————————213

Speaking About Management——————215

Speaking About Doing Work———————217

Speaking About Vexations————————222

Speaking About Desires—————————225

Speaking About Social Customs—————228

Section Two: About Religion

Speaking About Cause and Effect————*232*

Speaking About Eliminating Disaster————*236*

Speaking About Superstition————————*238*

Speaking About Faith——————————*242*

Speaking About Imitating Buddha's Behavior

————————————————————*247*

Speaking About Unselfish Giving————*254*

Speaking About the Practice of Buddhist

Rules——————————————————*257*

Speaking About Karmaic Hindrances————*274*

Speaking About Converting————————*278*

Appendix————————————————*281*

Part 1

The Dawn of Still

Thoughts

Chapter One: Allow Life to Function Always Like a Spring Day
(*The Goal of Life*)

N o matter where it is we want to go, there will always have to be a starting point and a goal. We should pursue our goals from the very beginning till the very end, never stopping halfway along the journey. It is more tiring, and even dangerous, to struggle in place in the middle of the road than it is to progress toward reaching the final goal. Mountain climbing is a fitting example. You must either stand at the bottom of the mountain, or climb in one breath to the very top. By stopping halfway up the mountain, you put yourself in danger of being hit by falling rocks.

W e will always encounter unfavorable situations, times of foggy or chilly weather that bring discomfort to our lives. Only if we remain calm and devoted to our goals, can all of life's calamities turn to warm sunshine in times of winter.

L ife is filled with changes. The existence of wisdom endures forever. The sphere of love is boundless. The power of the spirit persists for always.

A profession is but a job for earning money. You punch the clock and try to complete your assignments on time in the office. But your spiritual career has nothing to do with being "on" or "off" duty. Throughout your life, you must strive ahead in your spiritual career as a compulsory task.

You must spend time, if you want to do something meaningful. To do so is a goal and an obligation for your life.

The span of life is but few decades, whereas one's intellectual life is eternal. Just as we give life to our children, we should also provide them with wonderful memories and a loving education. In this way, we can make our intellectual lives immortal.

Those who become Buddhists must have the goal of life in their hearts to keep them from going astray on their life's voyage. Having a goal in life is essential to becoming a Buddhist. Those who lead others to convert to Buddhism must assume the responsibility of leading the way by turning on the lamp in the lighthouse when converts lose their direction in life.

Allow Life to Function Always Like a Spring Day

A truly living life is one that functions endlessly. You will be full of the energy of life when you let your life function always like a spring day. Do not let your conscience hibernate.

T he reason the world, the nation, the society, and families cannot achieve a peaceful and friendly state, is because we only fight to survive. We fail to discover the significance of survival.

Chapter Two: The Starting Point of Success
(Speaking of Perseverance)

R esolution is the starting point of success, and it is something we need in life. Resolution is hope, and it is indispensable if we want to have a successful career. All Buddhas, regardless of their generation, achieved the goal of becoming a Buddha by first having the quality of determination. Without resolution there cannot be hope. And we accomplish nothing, if we do not have hope.

uddhism puts equal emphasis on the importance of resolution-making and action-taking. To sit and talk idly will never make our wishes come true. We must be resolved to perform with practical action.

 ake a resolution that is beneficial to the whole of mankind, and try to make it come true with constant action.

 n order to save or deliver all beings, we need to make a strong resolution and be determined for showing care and concern for all beings.

 e should make a great resolution and cultivate it through unflinching perseverance, while acting gently and carefully.

Chapter Three: A Sweet Fountain in a Dessert
(The Spirit of Religion)

S ome people do not understand the Philosophy of Buddha. They assume that the people who need help from religion are only those who are facing big troubles and are too weak to resolve problems by themselves. To them, Buddhism appears to be passive and a form of escapism. This, of course, is incorrect. Religion -- and Buddhism in particular -- is just as necessary for the people who have the strength of knowledge, and who are determined to investigate the true meaning of the universe and of life.

To live freely and with ease, we must have religious spirit and a goal in life.

To be a Buddhist, you must have the resolve of an athlete. You will surely reach the finish line, the territory of Buddha, as long as you are willing to run.

Religion is the sole force that cheers us and brings a sense of rebirth to our personalities.

All human affairs are reciprocal. Our lives will be full of truth, goodness and beauty if we treat other people with sincerity and consider things with an open mind.

STILL THOUGHTS

A true Buddhist will not only worship Buddha, but will imitate Buddha as well. He will try to imitate Buddha's grand wisdom and mercy.

T he Philosophy of Buddha can be an effective medicine for curing life's diseases. All beings in the world share the same sufferings, which have been inflicted either by natural disasters or manmade holocausts caused by physical and mental disharmony. It is the Philosophy of Buddha that can bring us to a state of harmony, both physically and spiritually.

T he true spirit of Buddhism lies in unselfishness. We should do everything possible to make all living creatures peaceful and happy. We should sacrifice our interests, if it is necessary, for others.

Chapter Four: The Personification of Mercy and Wisdom
(*The Heart of a Bodhisattva*)

We should select our religious belief with a rational heart, and then pursue that belief via the guidance of truth. Each of us has a Bodhisattva's heart, which possesses the qualities of mercy and wisdom. We can trace these good qualities to a Bodhisattva, as well as to our very human nature.

A Bodhisattva is a merciful person, one who constantly performs beneficence for others. Wherever he goes, he never feels frightened. We in society should act as does a Bodhisattva. Be kind to others,

11

and you will never be offensive and will always encounter beautiful things.

A Bodhisattva's compassion is boundless, broad enough to accommodate the entire universe. He extends his love to all beings, asking nothing in return. He is content with what he has and, unlike ordinary people, wants only wisdom.

I nside each of us exists kindness and tranquillity, the nature of Buddha. Yet only when we develop our conscience to the extent of saving and helping other people, will we be acting as does a Bodhisattva.

I f you seek to achieve the goal of becoming a Bodhisattva, you must undergo spiritual trials and tribulations. You must be brave enough to face hard work, cultivate an unwavering perseverance, and strive toward the objective.

The love of a Bodhisattva is like a glass of water. It is clean and colorless. You can see all the way through it from the very top to the very bottom. It is "a love as pure as clean water."

The wooden and clay Bodhisattvas for worship are not the real Bodhisattva. A real Bodhisattva is a kind person who can work, speak and eat.

You must be determined to reach the goal of becoming a Bodhisattva. A Bodhisattva will do what he has to do, no matter how difficult it can be, and he will do so with delight.

We must face challenges bravely if we want to learn a Bodhisattva's wisdom. By remaining as calm and persevering as did Buddha some 2,500 years ago, we can endure our own stresses and thorns of difficulty.

STILL THOUGHTS

The value of life lies in your function, not in the image you display. The image you project does not have any value at all.

The wooden and stone Buddhas and Bodhisattvas in temples are not the real Buddha that can inspire us. They merely help calm us so we can concentrate our minds on the study of the Philosophy of Buddha. The truly inspirational Buddha can only be found in our hearts.

We should express happiness for the accomplishments of others. It is a Bodhisattva's mindset to regard others' achievements as his own. We will live happily when we always strive to be kind and helpful to all living beings.

To a Bodhisattva, life is but a play performed on a stage. We all are actors or actresses playing different roles on the stage of life.

Chapter Five: We Came Nakedly Into the World
(*Making Good Use of Our Bodies*)

We should cherish the body, since it can help us accomplish meritorious deeds. We must make good use of our bodies, for all our achievements are accumulated gradually through the use of bodily actions.

As disciples of Buddha, we should imitate the spirit of Buddha by helping others and sharing their happiness and troubles. A successful, meaningful life can only be realized if we are thoughtful toward other people.

STILL THOUGHTS

We cannot avoid the life cycle of birth, aging, illness and death. We cannot escape the torture of illness. Buddha has said, I am a good doctor. I can diagnose and prescribe for a patient. But it is beyond my ability to determine whether he will listen to me or not. If you know that you are sick, you must listen to the doctor's advice to care for your illness.

There are generally two ways people treat their bodies. You can love it too much, as if it was too valuable to be utilized. Or, you can despise it to excess, as if it was too filthy to be cared for. However, if you make good use of your body, you can reach great achievements and realize the Philosophy of Buddha.

We came nakedly into the world on the first day of our lives, and after decades of hard work we can take nothing with us at the moment we leave this world. Life in this way is just so simple; we come and we go empty-handed.

Loitering away each day turns us into "consumers" of life. Only by working energetically can we make the transformation into a "creator" for living our lives. We waste our lives when we live idly. We can make them much more enjoyable by endeavoring to be kind and helpful to others.

Make good use of your body to do the best you can in helping others promote the Philosophy of Buddha. Guide people in the right direction by keeping your body in good health.

All our behaviors throughout life, whether good or evil, are accumulated gradually.

Chapter Six: The River of Love Can Be as Dangerous as a Tidal Wave
(*Speaking of Love and Romance*)

I f a person indulges in excessive self-love, he can hardly avoid arguing with others and becoming suspicious of their intentions. To him, an ordinary comment may sound ironical, and he may view common behavior as an insult to his dignity. Being so suspicious and vulnerable, life to him is but a painful endurance.

L ove is a tremendous power. Love can be beneficial to all beings, if you give unselfishly. But it can damage your spiritual existence, if you keep it totally for yourself.

Y ou must first turn on the light that is in your heart, for it can lead and inspire others. Something more than ability is necessary for becoming a true leader -- sincerity. You must accommodate others with an open heart, and try to give your love to all living beings.

T o sufficiently practice the Philosophy of Buddha on earth, we must take action to purify society. But before we try to purify the hearts of others, we must first purify our own. What is purification? It means to cultivate the clean love of Buddha. And what is the love of Buddha? It means to express your love to all living beings in the world, asking nothing in return.

T here is a common disease in today's society, and it is a loveless disease. We should start, one and all, to add more love to our society. We can first fill our own heart with love and harmony, and then the rest of society.

A loving and merciful heart suits the nature of women. It is a wife's duty to guide her husband's journey in the right direction, and it is a mother's duty to do things that are kindly and beneficial to others.

S ome people only look after the members of their own family. But people of this sort become upset easily when family members fail to meet expectations.

I t is fortunate to be a loving person, and to be loved by another. But our love for others should be as pure as a glass of water. A person who gives love should ask nothing in return, and the recipient of love should not be greedy. In this way, both the giver and the receiver can dwell in happiness and ease.

A river of love can be as dangerous as a tidal wave, an ocean of lust can be as treacherous as a hurricane. It is painful when you fail to attract the one you love, yet it is even more painful when you succumb easily to other temptations after winning the one you love.

T he divorce rate for the middle-aged in Taiwan is rising rapidly, causing numerous problems for our society. We should try to help troubled families by nurturing healthy family ethics in our own homes first.

L ove the ones you should love, and it will be a great love. You need to cultivate a good feeling with your loved ones every day. When the relationship turns sour, you must move one step backward to accept reality with an open heart. This, then, can be called a wise love.

T he carnal desires of ordinary people can never be satisfied. These people are always running after material comforts and carnal pleasures in life. This attitude is the source of their unhappiness.

A pure love is the condition of loving regardless of time, place or person. No matter how long love lasts, how far distant the loved one is, or what ethnic or religious group he belongs to, love unconditionally. We should offer our pure love even to people with whom we do not have a special relationship, and we should have the compassion to share in the unhappiness of others.

W e should strive to imitate Buddha's love for all living beings. What Buddha did, we should do. Buddha loved, so should we. Since Buddha sacrificed whatever he had in order to love all beings, we should devote our time and energy to achieving the spiritual goal of helping all living beings.

The River of Love Can Be as Dangerous as a Tidal Wave

T he kind of love promoted by Buddhism breaks through the limited bonds so that your love can be offered to all living beings. We should regard the calamities suffered by all living beings as our own pains.

Chapter Seven: We Should Do More Than Simply Talk a Lot
(Speaking on the Cultivation of Morality)

The reason why a man has two ears, two eyes, two hands and two feet, yet only one mouth, is because he should listen, observe and work more, while talking but a little. A Chinese philosopher once noted, "A frog croaking day and night is detestable, while a rooster's crowing is useful." A few significant words can carry a great meaning, while meaningless talk only makes others drowsy. It is more likely that we will achieve our goal of morality cultivation by busying ourselves with carrying out what we have learned. We should do more than just sit there excessively talking.

T he various methods of morality cultivation, such as Zen meditation and the chanting of sutras, serve the function of strengthening our mind-concentration. The purpose of morality cultivation is to eliminate any artificiality within us for increasing the genuine and the real.

I t is not difficult to make a pure and clean society. We should start toward achieving this goal by first doing good deeds. In order to make the whole society beautiful, each of us must begin by making our own effort. If we combine all the beauty of individual achievements, then the entire society will become beautiful. If we long for the fulfilling world of a Bohdisattva, then we should start to behave like a Bohdisattva.

T he effort to cultivate our virtue must be achieved through daily conduct, and should be done carefully, patiently. Only by behaving in

25

accordance with the Philosophy of Buddha, can we realize the goal of imitating Buddha and cultivating virtue.

B efore saving the world, we must first save our own hearts. A sincere heart is the basis of proper behavior. As Confucius once said, In order to unify the world in peace, we must first cultivate ourselves, have a good family, and govern our country well. If we want to have a harmonious family, we must improve our own morality. Then, our harmonious family can be an example for others. When each family becomes harmonious, we can have a peaceful and happy society.

H ow do we measure one's moral accomplishment? It exists inside, but one can radiate it outwardly through daily behavior. A man's behavior demonstrates his moral accomplishment.

We must be careful with what we say. We have to give sufficient thought to what we are about to say to see if our words will be reasonable, inspirational, and of benefit for helping others solve their problems.

Just as we all have different faces, we also have different characters. In order to cultivate our morality and practice Buddhist conduct, we must try to work and live smoothly with others. We have to get along with our fellowman, and always treat others nicely.

A person will never do immoral or unreasonable things, if he has a strong sense of shame. When a person wants to cultivate morality and imitate Buddha, he must first cultivate a sense of shame.

A person of fortitude is one who can tolerate insult, and who cannot be knocked down by physical pain or mental anguish. Tolerance is the cornerstone of success.

I n order to practice the Philosophy of Buddha, we should enlighten not only ourselves, but others as well. We should constantly cultivate our wisdom and feelings of mercy, never offending or slandering others.

M an often harms others for the sake of self-love. Buddha, therefore, teaches us that rule number one for reaching the goal of morality cultivation is to "never harm others."

O ur society is composed of a large group of people. Being good to yourself when no one else is good cannot be said to be good. We must be grateful of one another, if we want to establish a good family and a good society.

A society's style stems from its type of family education. Our family education is based on each of us cultivating morality. If we do a good job in morality cultivation, and take good care of our families, then we will create a peaceful society.

T he cultivation of morality actually means a refining of one's personality and a correcting of one's bad behavior. In other words, one should bear in mind a sense of shame. Show me a person who does not know how to search his soul for self-examination, and I will show you a man who does not possess the sense of shame. He can never behave himself, and it is impossible to converse with him regarding the refinement of personality.

T hose who can tolerate the faults of others are people of great fortune and intuition.

We should always act carefully, but not narrow-mindedly, in our daily conduct.

We should always bring our frame of mind into harmony, cultivate a healthy life-concept, conquer grief, and weed through the vanities of self-benefit and desire. We should not be greedy when possessing something, and we should not be frustrated upon losing it. Only by being as such, are we able to free ourselves from worldly worries.

If we want to accomplish something important in the world, we must first cultivate virtue and sublimate our personality. Above all, whenever or wherever, we must respect others.

Being members of society, we often encounter many unfriendly people and complicated matters. As we learn to deal with them, we cultivate morality and virtue.

Even though we may not be hurting others' bodies, we can sometimes tarnish their good reputation by carelessly spreading nasty gossip. The latter is the worst of the two crimes. Physical pain is temporary, while a blemish on a man's image may twist his personality for the rest of his life.

We can never rely on the help of others for cultivating morality. We can only enjoy the fruits of enlightenment by our own endeavors. We should not forget that without pain there cannot be gain.

STILL THOUGHTS

I f we want to imitate Buddha's behavior, we must be concerned about other people and their business. We should not care too much about what we have gained or lost, and we should be brave when facing difficulty and challenges.

W e must be honest and sincere when talking or doing business with others. Furthermore, our own viewpoints should be based on reason and logic when we discuss the Philosophy of Buddha with others. We should not frighten away the ordinary with stories of miracles and mystery. Only by promoting Buddhism through a healthy, reasonable approach, can we upgrade our fellowman's Buddhist knowledge to lead him to the right road.

T here are three important points devotees and students of Buddhism must remember. First, you must have a pure and innocent heart like that of a child. A straightforward attitude is a necessity for enlightenment. Second, you need to cultivate a camel's spirited endurance. You should work as diligently and patiently as a camel. Third, you should be as brave as a lion to improve yourself via that bravery.

"Penetrating truth together" means that the Buddhist students in a group help one another enter a realm of understanding by discussing the Philosophy of Buddha, eliminating worldly mannerisms, and nurturing a pure and innocent heart like that of the Buddha.

"Coursing together" means that Buddhist students in a group help one another correct mistakes. A mistake should be perceived as a warning signal for avoiding the same mistake in the future.

"Trying hard to practice the Philosophy of Buddha" means to purify one's heart, diminish one's worldly desires, and cultivate a strong will power for enduring difficulty and challenges.

T hose who want to practice the Philosophy of Buddha must exhibit the following four cardinal principles in their daily conduct: be aware of your words, be aware of your behavior, be aware of your manner, and be aware of your heart.

F irst, to be aware of your words, you should not carelessly elaborate upon the meaning of Buddha's philosophy. Each uttered word from your mouth must be encouraging and inspirational. What you say should convey Buddha's philosophy.

S econd, to be aware of your behavior, behave properly in your daily conduct. Your virtue and morality will be revealed through your behavior.

T hird, to be aware of your manner, you should always be gentle, yet unyielding and serious, when dealing with others. By doing so, you will make yourself popular, and will avoid the risk of others taking advantage of you. "Be gentle yet serious, be authoritative yet not too rude in your manner," Confucius once said. "Be gracious, simple, earnest, modest and courteous," he added. If your behavior is frivolous and insensitive, you will attract nothing but despise and humiliation. We should therefore keep gentleness and authoritativeness in balance.

F orth, to be aware of your heart, try to be understanding, thoughtful and forgiving toward others. You will make yourself popular among friends by nurturing within yourself a heart of gold.

A bstention, calm and wisdom are three necessities for practicing the Philosophy of Buddha. We should not be tempted by worldly desires, and should be able to abstain from selfishness, greed and the eagerness for fame. We should remain calm and resolute when in trouble. We should be able to turn an unfavorable situation into a pleasant one by using wisdom.

T hose who want to practice the Philosophy of Buddha must have an easy, tranquil mind. "When a bird flies across the sky, it will leave no trail on the white clouds. When a carp jumps out of the stream, it will draw no marks on the surface of the water." We should not worry about things that happened long ago.

T he Saints keep no dreams" is an old Chinese saying. When a Saint wakes up, he lets go of all his dreams and immediately faces real life. He devotes his energy to work, not dwelling on dreams.

W hen a man lives in fear and anxiety, he consequently loses confidence or becomes trapped in a lifestyle of cowardice and escapism.

We Should Do More Than Simply Talk a Lot

We must always bear one rule in mind: we must act justly and be upright for the sake of Buddhism and for all living beings. We should be tolerant of others' misunderstandings and unfair accusations, as long as we can honestly face our own self-examining.

Chapter Eight: The Proper Way to Manage Finances
(Speaking About Money and Finance)

M any people in the world commit crimes to collect treasures. "The desire to obtain money is the source of trouble," goes an old Chinese saying. To realize the goal of imitating Buddha's behavior, we need to cultivate a heart of mercy with happiness, so that we will be willing to give unselfishly. The money we earn is but something we can use to buy the things that we need in our daily life.

A lot of people are manipulative in their efforts by flattering important people so they can obtain fame and money for themselves. How painful to behave in this way. To make ourselves happier, we would do better to treat others with honesty, and use our money in a proper way.

G iving to charity is equivalent to cultivating good fortune for yourself. You will be no better than the poor, if you become a miser by depositing all your treasure in a bank and refusing to donate to charity. You might damage your health, or even cause trouble for your country and fellow countrymen, if you continue to abuse your fortune. You should use your money properly while you are still alive and able to do so. It is a good opportunity, when you are able to cultivate fortune and morality by using your money for things meaningful.

We should manage our money properly. This can be compared to sitting around a fire in winter. If we sit at a proper distance, the fire will give us warmth. Otherwise, we will become burnt. Fame and fortune can also be likened to a piece of ice. You can cool off from the summer heat by putting the ice in a glass of tea, but you will suffer frostbite if you hold it too long in your hands. People sometimes become confused by money. They are willing to be hurt by fame and money, even though they are aware these two can be dangerous.

Buddha tells us to divide our income into four portions. We can therefore spend one-fourth to support our parents, one-fourth on our children's education, another portion on family expense, and the last share on public welfare.

Money sometimes brings us trouble, but it can also help us save people. We should control money, not be controlled by it.

T hose with money and power should learn to limit their desires. Otherwise, they will meet with nothing but anguish. People who cannot see through the vanity generated by fame and wealth will live a corrupt spiritual life, and will have an empty heart.

Chapter Nine: To Light a Lamp in the Dark
(*Speaking About Imitating Buddha's Behavior*)

T he most important job for people who want to imitate Buddha's behavior is to cultivate a heart of mercy. Without doing so, you cannot possess the spirit of Buddhism.

P eople who want to imitate Buddha's behavior must look at life and death without bias. Make the most of your life and do your work well. Only then can you achieve harmony in family and society for avoiding natural disasters and manmade calamities.

To imitate Buddha's behavior, we must first maintain a heart full of delight. In order to do so, we must behave properly and reflect constantly upon our actions. We will be at ease after examining our conscience and finding no big mistakes.

It is merely a practice of superstition if we only believe in Buddha while refusing to imitate Buddha's kindness and mercy. You cannot call yourself a Buddhist if you only worship Buddha. You will be acting like Buddha if you imitate Buddha's virtue, mercy and wisdom while seeking to understand yourself and the essence of the universe.

In order to maintain good judgment, we should understand the vicissitudes of life with intellect and reason. We can then live happily, regardless of our social status or financial situation. We can also eliminate our concern for gains and losses.

STILL THOUGHTS

Chinese people by tradition clean their homes and repaint the walls at the time of the Chinese New Year. Having decided to imitate Buddha's behavior, we should remove the old dirt in our hearts everyday, just as we clean our homes for the new year.

Some people constantly create troubles and prolong their faults because they have failed to conquer human weakness. Those who imitate Buddha's behavior understand this situation and strive to break away from this kind of regretful life. They seek to purify their minds by studying the Philosophy of Buddha.

Buddhists believe in the concept of cause and effect, and that good fortune comes as a reward. Wealth is not the only factor to create good fortune. We can help create fortunate rewards for ourselves if we can constantly extend our care and concerns to others.

Both Buddha and Jesus Christ came into the world for the sake of saving us. In order to achieve their goal, they, too, had to face the realities of life and overcome many difficulties. We can accomplish our goals lightheartedly once successful in grasping the significance of human nature and our own duty.

"**P**erforming countless meritorious deeds" is an expression used frequently by Buddhists. Its meaning is that as Buddhists we should do what we must and, above all, ask nothing in return.

In order to imitate Buddha's behavior, we should do the best we can to remain calm and to disarm the hostilities of others.

In order to behave like Buddha, we should not only increase our knowledge, but also implement what we understand as appropriate in our minds.

e can never extend our lives of wisdom if we evade duty and live idly.

 e will accomplish nothing if we fail to concentrate our minds on the one important task. Be sure to make your selection carefully, and then perform it resolutely.

 e imitate Buddha's behavior for the sake of helping all living creatures. The reason why we should act sincerely toward others is because we can then get things done readily.

 oung Buddhists often indulge themselves in the reading of sutras. But it is more significant if they can apply the wisdom they have learned from sutras to the actions of practical life.

We should start to imitate Buddha's behavior by performing well in each day's basic work. Our meritorious contributions accumulate through our daily conducts. The earlier we start to cultivate our virtue, the sooner we will see it reach fruition.

A most enjoyable life is when you feel that you are needed.

Before imitating Buddha's behavior, we are often dominated by worldly desires. We can never satisfy those desires, just like we can never humidify an arid desert with only a few drops of water. After learning Buddha's wisdom, we are able to limit our desires for material things, and thus devote our time and energy to cultivating our conscience and knowledge. Moreover, we are able to march gratefully on the proper road of life.

STILL THOUGHTS

People who imitate Buddha's behavior know how to get along with others, how to resolve confrontations, and how to accept the shortcomings of others. These people never criticize others behind their backs, and that is how they make themselves admirable and lovable.

Human affairs are not as complicated as we may have once thought. Do not forget that we are all members of the human society.

Accepting sutras means we apply what we have learned from the Philosophy of Buddha to practical life.

Those who want to imitate Buddha's behavior must possess a heart that is motivated to search for the truth. If you fail to do so, you will not only destroy your heart of morality, but also extinguish your lamp of wisdom. Be sure to watch out for your thoughts, and do not let what happens in the outside world extinguish your lamp of wisdom.

T he significance in imitating Buddha's behavior lies in nurturing a heart of equality. In this, you will be able to treat others as equals, and will make yourself happier when you are with others. If you accept others with the kind heart of Buddha, then everyone will become as kindly as a Buddha.

W e must first have confidence and faith before we start to imitate Buddha's behavior. It is best for the new disciples of Buddha to ask themselves, "Why do I believe in Buddha? What is the significance of Buddhist sutras?"

T he meaning of imitating Buddha's behavior lies in getting along well with others.

Chapter Ten: Personal Growth in a Challenging World
(*Speaking About the Hardships of Life*)

B e grateful when you are undergoing difficulties, because they will help you grow.

O nly by enduring the tribulations of life, can we become great.

O nly few people realize that life is filled with changes. We can hardly predict if we will be as healthy or fortunate tomorrow as we are today.

Many people intend to perform good acts. However, they never take action for implementing their good intentions. This is why they live a life full of regret.

T he vicissitudes of our lives are based on the changes of our profession, career, and spiritual career.

A profession is a job for earning money, while a career is the expansion of a profession. Take an entrepreneur for example: he pursues fame and money, yet at the same time provides working opportunities for other people. His career assists the functioning of our social economy.

O ur dedication to profession or career is merely a limited demonstration of our capabilities. Each of us should have strong willpower for doing something that benefits others. Without this, we degrade our lives to the level of that of dogs, swine and other life

51

forms.

Buddha teaches us that there is little difference between human beings and other life forms. However, unlike the other life forms that care only about themselves or their own species, we as human beings should imitate Buddha's merciful behavior in order to save and deliver all living beings. This is known as our spiritual career.

Do not speak too often about a sense of frustration or inability. You must overcome these problems, even though they may be as hard as pieces of rock. Besides, the task might not be as hard as you once thought.

Suicide is wrong for three reasons: First, a person who commits suicide destroys the body given to him by his parents. Second, suicide is inherently sinful. Third, a person who commits suicide abandons his responsibilities to his parents, spouse, and children.

D o not resort to complaining about friction and disagreement between you and your friends. Try to replace the complaints with understanding and forgiveness.

B e confident to do whatever is proper, and do not quit along this task even though you may suffer setbacks. Buddha says, "Those who come into my place will no longer be poor, and those who leave my place will no longer be rich." The poor are helped by the rich, and the rich give their extra money to the poor. If you are equipped with a Buddhist's courage and confidence, you will be able to face difficulties and illness with a delightful heart.

P eople tend to lose themselves in an easy life. It is therefore lucky when we occasionally face set-backs and troubles, for they wake up our sleeping conscience and help us grow.

W e can eliminate the calamities in our lives by performing our duties well. It is useless to pray to Buddha for his help. Instead, we should imitate Buddha's behavior, so that we can help ourselves and others.

W e reap as we have sown. Do not wait until you are hospitalized before thinking of the importance of caring for your body. By then, only your children can look after you, though they cannot endure the pain for you. We should perform good acts for others while we are healthy. By doing so now, we will reap a good harvest in the future.

A delightful heart is able to suffer through the unfavorable results, blowing the dark clouds back into the past.

A sk yourself if you can face yourself without a sense of guilt when severely criticized by others. If the answer is affirmative, you will see all criticism slide right off your shoulder.

F eel grateful when you are held back by someone else, for their doing so will help you grow.

B eing Buddhists, we should devote our time and energy to serving others. We should cultivate a spirit of perseverance by enduring what others cannot, by giving up what the others refuse to give, and by completing what others are unable to complete.

Chapter Eleven: Healthy Yet Useless
(*Speaking About Wrongdoing*)

t would certainly affect your personal life if you did not have two feet. But a healthy man can also face trouble that he brings to himself, and to others, if he continues to commit wrongdoings.

A man with two hands that refuses to work is no better than a man without hands.

healthy man should always behave properly, otherwise he will fall into an unbearable situation. This is worse than being an unhealthy man.

 devil is an evil spirit that prevents people from doing good things. The devil of the outside world is not as horrible as the one inside your heart. The devil inside your heart can disturb your sense of peace and love so that you harm others and ruin yourself.

Chapter Twelve: Many Grains of Rice Make a Bushel

(*Many a Little Makes a Mickle*)

Many grains of rice make a bushel. Do not throw away even one grain of rice, lest you will never be able to gather a full bushel. Many drops of water make a river. We should not waste even one drop of water.

Your countless meritorious contributions are accumulated little by little throughout your life.

T**he** meritorious deeds performed by a group of people are greater than those by a single person. The light from a big candle illuminates a larger space than does a small candle. But when hundreds of thousands of small candles are lit, their light can illuminate every corner of our society.

W**e** should have self-respect, and at the same time be humble. None of us can single-handedly govern the whole country.

O**pportunity** knocks only once. We should grasp every chance to do something good, since our lives fluctuate rapidly. When all the good little things you have performed accumulate, they collectively stand as a great meritorious deed. Do not delay making donations until you become rich. You should do whatever you can today.

Chapter Thirteen: Don't Choose a Venomous Snake as Your Companion (*The Five Poisons of Greed, Anger, Delusion, Arrogance and Suspicion*)

T he worry in your mind is more dangerous than your enemies. Do not let your conscience fall asleep. Otherwise, your heart will be occupied by the evils of slaughter, robbery, debauchery and absurd desires.

T he worry in your mind is like a venomous snake that will bite you if you touch it. We must eliminate senseless worry, so that we can practice Buddhist virtue.

Anger will damage a man by destroying his good manner and attitude of delight toward others. The strong emotion of anger will not only tarnish a man's good reputation, but also erase all the meritorious deeds he previously accomplished. Anger is more violent than a blazing fire. All the valuable articles burned out by fire can be restored with money. But you can never purchase back your reputation or good personality once you ruin them.

Greed is what brings disaster and calamity to our lives. Our greed not only brings us pain, but also leads others astray toward indulging in evil ways. It not only makes us lose fortune and honor in this life, but also brings unhappiness to our next life.

Many people in our society make themselves unhappy because of their worldly desires. Such desires can easily ruin a man's fortitude and good reputation. The strong desire for achieving fame and wealth can destroy our families and cause us to fall into an abyss of worry and anguish. As human beings, we are indeed harmed by our desires. This is why Buddha teaches us to understand the dangers of material desires, so that we can have a clear conscience.

When people live in extreme extravagant, they become befuddled. They believe their lives will always be extravagant, failing to understand that the moon will not be full all the time; neither will the flowers be always in bloom nor the beautiful scenery remain unchanged. Life, in fact, is filled with unexpected changes.

Commonplace people tend to be greedy. When they obtain money and power, they want even more. When a man of this sort has a beautiful wife, he still wants a pretty mistress. When a woman of this sort has a kindly husband, she desires to make him submissive. When her son is well-behaved, she demands that he ace every course in school. Consequently, the commonplace people live unsatisfactory lives, pursuing fame, money, love and everything else. How painful it is to be this way.

T here are four invisible demons in our hearts: invisible disaster-prone stupidity, the invisible sword of jealousy, the invisible devil of suspicion, and the invisible prison as the biased faith of evil. These four can destroy good-natured intentions.

B uddhist philosophy is actually very simple. You can enlighten your mind and realize the Buddha-nature inherent in your heart by eliminating the bad habits of greed, anger and delusion. Commonplace people, however, have complexity in their minds. This is why Buddha has 84,000 ways for coping.

M any people are hypocritical in manner, due to their greed. In order to love in a truly happy life, we must be free of worry.

A thief may not be able to steal all your valuables in only one minute's time. But once you become angry, the thief within your heart steals away all your previous meritorious contributions in just one second.

G reed, anger, delusion, arrogance and suspicion are the five illnesses of human beings. There are also five desires that can bring us unhappiness: the desire for wealth, wanton sex, fame, lavish food and idle sleeping. It will be easier for you to help deliver other people, if you remove these five desire-driven illnesses.

C ommonplace people often arrogantly assume that they will gain something in return if they are willing to give. When these people donate money to the poor, they actually gain in return nothing but disappointment. This is because a donation performed without a sense of heartfelt charity can never bring you a happiness equal to that of a meritorious deed.

The three poisons of greed, anger and delusion will not only bring trouble and calamity to our families, but also ruin the whole of our society and nation.

We should view the people around us as mirrors for self-reflection, so that we can imitate their good behavior and avoid repeating their mistakes.

Chapter Fourteen: Tolerance
(*To Bear Disgrace and Insult*)

W e will never be able to achieve anything great if we cannot bear insults while performing our duties conscientiously. We must be able to endure physical stress and mental harassment in order to put Buddhism into practice and to learn the Philosophy of Buddha.

T olerance means that we utilize a delightful manner for enduring everything disgraceful caused by our past actions.

The true spirit of Nirvana lies in a peaceful mentality that can accommodate all sorts of people and events, and cannot be mentally dominated by the changing environment.

A truly successful man must have a propensity for accommodating others, and be such that others are willing to accommodate him.

Try to maintain a still mind when you busy yourself with work. In order to live happily, we must maintain our conscience when we are busy, and not let our morality fall asleep when we have time for relaxing.

Be sure to keep calm and remain tolerant when you and your colleagues have dissimilar ideas or interests in the office. In addition, you must not utter an unkind word to them.

I n order to keep a clean, still mind, we must cultivate a capacity for tolerance similar to that of a saint. If you fail to do so, you will never be enlightened, no matter how sincere and frequent is your worship of Buddha.

T olerance is something that can help you perform good deeds and put Buddhism into practice. Those who observe the Buddhist commandments may not always be those that are able to tolerate insults; but those who tolerate insults are definitely able to observe the commandments. We can therefore conclude that it is more difficult to be tolerant. If each of us can be tolerant of others, then our society will be more harmonious. A man will be able to strive for progress and be self-supporting if he can tolerate insults. Tolerance is the key to one's sublimation of morality. There will be no dispute if each of us can be equipped with the virtue of tolerance. Tolerance is indeed a necessity of Observing the Buddist Commandments.

I
f you can always bear the shortcomings of others, you will find that nothing is difficult and no one is seen as being disgusting. Buddhists believe in the phenomenon of "cause and effect." Thus, by being nice to others you in turn will be treated nicely.

I
t would be difficult to imitate Buddha's behavior if you cannot tolerate insult and slandering. Do not be angry when you are ill-treated by others. You should be grateful to them, since they are the ones who will let everyone else know how nice and graceful you are. In the same way, we can never appreciate a Bodhisattva's loving heart if there are no suffering living beings for whom he can show love and caring. We should accept insults and slander as if there were honeydew.

Chapter Fifteen: Do Not Plant Poison Ivy in Your Heart
(*Speaking About Mentality*)

A delightful heart is like a springtime breeze that cheers up the people around you.

W e all had a kind heart like that of the Shakyamuni's (Buddha) when we came to the world. However, our hearts changed and became less pure as we met various environmental influences. That is why we need to cultivate virtue for having our hearts restored.

Our hearts are easily influenced by the changing environment. But we must cultivate a persistent heart capable of outlasting any difficulty, just as constant dripping water can wear away a stone. We Buddhists call this persistent heart "resolution."

It is nothing to pity when you lose a large sum of money. What is really pitiful, is when you lose your kind and pure nature and yet remain unaware of its absence. Each of us has a pure and innocent (Buddist) nature, which is gradually tarnished by worry and stupidity.

We should be vigilant in times of peace, yet prepared for any problem that should suddenly come by.

New converts of Buddhism must train themselves, physically and mentally, to be strong enough for putting Buddhism into practice, and

71

brave enough for facing any difficult challenge. Their minds must be capable of remaining calm and still when in a turbulent situation.

We should learn to adjust our mentality in accordance with the age of the people to whom we are speaking. By doing so, we also become good listeners.

Buddha teaches us to be content with what we have, and to obey the law. We can have a calm heart and live happily by doing so.

We need to put equal emphasis on study and practical implementation. A devotee of Buddhism can hardly erase all his worries, but he can still perform meritorious deeds if determined to help deliver other living beings. That is why we say, "The way to enlightenment is paved with worries."

Our human minds are more destructive than lethal weapons, since the latter was created by the former.

Only by bringing our bodies and minds into harmony, can we cultivate a merciful and wise mind for helping and leading others.

All the wealth, power and fame we can gain throughout life is difficult to keep. We still feel empty upon gaining them. True fortune and happiness is stored in a heart full of mercy, kindness and love. You do not need to have a lot of money or power in order to have this sort of heart. Even so, this type of heart makes you stronger and more resolute.

There is no need to be afraid of submerged reefs along life's voyage if we remain honest and devoted to the people around us.

STILL THOUGHTS

You will never accomplish anything great if you fail to concentrate your mind on your work. Be sure to eliminate all random thoughts in order to have a clear mind.

At the very moment we wish to do something, we should examine our intentions to see whether they are rooted in fame and self-interest. By doing so, we can keep our hearts uplifted to a state of harmony and peace.

The full moon casts a brilliant silver sheen that spans the heavens. It brings a sense of peace to Earth. Our minds can be as luminous and tranquil as the moon-lit sky, if we do our utmost to cultivate morality. We do not need to study every inspirational word that Buddha said 2,500 years ago. We can gain much wisdom by fully understanding one or two of the sentences that he said.

A heart is like a piece of good natural land. If we keep it free of dirt and weeds, the land will bear the flowers of wisdom, which will not only beautify our lives, but also help purify society. If we maintain a clean mind, we will then enjoy a clean national territory. We should protect our minds from invasion by the three poisons of greed, anger and delusion. We should protect the world from being destroyed by disasters and pollution. We should keep society free from the damage wrought by violence.

I f you do not plow a piece of land, it soon will be covered with weeds. If you do not plant good fortune in the field of your heart, you will soon become foolish. We should therefore do good things every day. We can turn a wasteland into a land of good fortune by eliminating evil thoughts and unnecessary worries from our minds.

STILL THOUGHTS

T he Sutra of Medicine describes many physical and mental diseases suffered by human beings. It refers not to the kind of pain when a person is disabled, but to real pain, that which exists when a man has an incomplete human nature. The disasters and crimes in our society are often the product of healthy men who unfortunately have unhealthy minds. A physically unhealthy man, if strong of mind, can set a good example for other people of his kind.

I f we want to remain happy, we should view human friction lightly. We can regard it as a sort of education, and in doing so we can learn about how to get along with others and how to deal with problems.

B eware of the unnecessary worries in our minds. They are like thieves, who will not only hurt others, but also ruin ourselves. When a malicious thought comes across your mind, the thief of worry becomes immediately present. He will not hesitate to destroy your kindness and insight.

W e can remove all the calamities faced by our society by each of us cultivating a kind heart within. When each of us has a kind heart, all the people of our society, and all of mankind around the world, can live together peacefully.

B uddha teaches us to bring our minds and bodies into harmony. He also tells us to fill our hearts with love, and not with anger or hatred. By doing so, we can be more forgiving and thoughtful toward others.

---

 e should convert our greedy hearts into contented ones, and try to be merciful and kind.

STILL THOUGHTS

Each of us, like Buddha himself, has a mine in our hearts that is rich in precious stones. The difference is that the Buddha's mine has already been opened, and all the deposits of uncut jade have been taken out and polished. On the other hand, the ordinary people are too lazy to exploit the deposits of jade in their mines. They do not know how to polish a precious stone.

We should be determined to use the fulfillment of love as a way to achieve what we really hope to complete in our lives. Then, all the great things we accomplish will become part of eternity.

Chapter Sixteen: A Sutra We Must Read
(*Talking About Family Ethics*)

Many problems in our families are related to wealth, lust and other desires and interests.

The family is the core of our lives. Even a bird has its own nest. How can we enjoy family happiness when the husband, wife and children live in different places. Nothing is more valuable than family ethics.

If we want to have a happy and harmonious family, we should support each member of our family with full blessings.

Parents should do their duty to raise their children. However, parents should not force their children to grow according to the pattern they have framed.

When a husband has more than enough to eat and wear, his wife should encourage him to do good things for others. It is also a wife's duty to regard her aged father-in-law and mother-in-law as her own parents, so that her husband will be able to relate with his patents without friction.

The way a husband and wife treat each other and talk to each other sets an example for their children to follow. A true Buddhist family puts a lot of emphasis on the importance of courtesy. Whatever we do, our manner must be polite, respectful and considerate. Love is something you should not require others to give to you. You should offer your love to other people unselfishly.

Our life is full of illness. The disharmony of our bodies is an illness, quarrelsome disorder in a family is another, and social turmoil is a third kind.

Our bodies are composed of various materials. Therefore, the demise of our bodies is normal. I, too, suffer from illness. However, I try to bear it without complaint. Though we might be physically weak, we can be spiritually strong.

Likewise, a family's spiritual and mental communication is more important than materialism. We must understand that a harmonious family can enjoy love and happiness even when it is impoverished.

81

STILL THOUGHTS

Materialism does not necessarily guarantee a happy family life.

I have heard many people say, "Taiwan's social order is bad and the living quality is deteriorating. I cannot help but want to emigrate to another country." Emigration is such a tiring matter; it is equivalent to transplanting a tree in a new place. It is unpredictable whether the tree will be as sturdy as it once was. It is very hard to adapt to a new environment with a different climate and strange soil.

In my opinion, emigration is passive and a form of escapism. It is better for us to make our own home more livable than to move to a foreign country. We should become more concerned about Taiwan's problems, such as environmental pollution, and treat all matters related to it as if they were our own responsibilities. It is merely a matter of time before the ugly duckling transforms into a beautiful swan.

Chapter Seventeen: March to Life's Tune
(*Speaking About Pure Love*)

A human being is earth's only living creature that not only knows how to help himself, but also knows how to help others. That is why we humans should not ask Buddha for help. Buddha can help the other creatures, not the humans of the world.

We should constantly re-examine what we have done in the past. Otherwise, we will exist merely as a group of mediocrities who do nothing but lounge around every day.

We will never feel that it is hard work to help others if we do it voluntarily. That is why we can easily see the virtue of sincerity within a volunteer.

It is a huge waste if we fool around every day. We should always do something beneficial for others, as does a Bodhisattva.

No one is an island. We cannot live alone. Being a member of a group known as society, we can hardly convince everyone else to sing the same song as we do all the time. The solution, therefore, is tolerance. Tolerance will help you expand your living space until it becomes as boundless as the sea and sky.

You will make yourself more popular if you behave naturally toward others. Our society will become more peaceful if each of us thinks of himself as a mediocrity.

Although everyone's life is valuable, some of us are more indispensable than others. What makes for this difference? It can be attributed to the contribution certain of us make to society.

When a man thinks only about his own interests, and when whatever he does is aimed only at achieving his own ends, his life is unimportant to others. However, when a man devotes his talent and time to helping others, his existence is certainly important to the people living around him. That is why we Chinese are accustomed to using the saying, "Some people's lives are as unimportant as feathers; some people's lives are as important as Mount Tai."

In modern society, no one can single-handedly get things done. We need the help of others in order to survive. For instance, we need to wear clothes, but even if you know how to make a suit or a dress, you still need the help of the person who can supply the raw materials. That is why we should be grateful to those who make our existence in this world possible. Be grateful!

O nce a man becomes lazy and just idles away his time, he also becomes dispirited. Life will soon become meaningless to him.

I t is a meaningless life if we let our bodies decay everyday without doing anything significant. We should gain wisdom through reading great philosophers' works, so that we can find out the significance of life as far as where we came from and where we shall go upon dying.

I t is natural to go through the life cycle of birth, decay, disease and death. It is wise for us to live happily and not worry about suffering through the life cycle.

A man with too much time on his hands will not enjoy his life. The busy man, however, is not troubled nor does he trouble others. A man who idles away his time is not a happy man. Also, we can see a lot of busy men who rush around from A to B and back again. But they do not seem happy either. Why? It is because these people have not performed any meaningful act. They are busy traveling, attending social activities, and sometimes even gambling. They do not enjoy a high level of satisfaction by doing these things.

We should not fool others with flattering words or behavior aimed only at reaching our own ends. To do so eventually hurts ourselves.

A happy life is not one that dwells in having only money and power, but one that gives and receives caring love.

To understand life in its entirety does not lead to pessimism. In fact, it is an endeavor of positive-ness and optimism. You will become more active in performing your work, and more content with what you have, once you perceive the good and the bad in life.

One of the most fulfilling sensations you can experience is when you try your best to do things beneficial to others.

When you help others voluntarily, you do so with-out complaint, even though you may face hard-ship and criticism. No matter how busy you are, you will always feel delighted.

Life will become boring and meaningless if it lacks love. And, it can even fester toward destructiveness if we only care about our own

relatives. We should extend our love to all living beings and, above all, ask nothing in return. The recipients of our love will be at ease, since they will be freed from any pressures.

W e cannot demonstrate merciful action without being polite. Through good manners, we can show the goodness, beauty and truth of humanity. We cannot separate wisdom from the virtue of humility. Wisdom helps us distinguish the good from the bad, while humility makes our lives more delighted.

O ur lives are like operas performed on a stage. Some have happy endings, some do not. It is not easy to judge whether the former ones are more touching than the latter ones. Only love is something that we can clearly count on. The most lasting aspect of love is mercy, which involves the noble spirit of unselfishness. Mercy is an invisible fortune and a guarantee of happiness.

STILL THOUGHTS

Buddha teaches us to be broad-minded, so that we can appreciate the fortune and happiness of others. This is the most positive attitude toward life that one can have.

Life is changeable and full of unexpected storms. So, be alert to the vicissitudes of life.

Life is like plays that are performed on a stage. Do not let the sad episodes bother you, since the theater curtain will go down before long. We should learn to replace our worrying with a merciful attitude toward others. This is a Bodhisattva's wisdom.

If a person is lazy, he will indulge in the evil life. We should be aware of this, and not let the gains and losses in life prevent us from marching toward life's goal -- helping others.

L ife is tough. Even if you are the luckiest person in the world, you cannot escape from climatic tortures. Yet, even though we must endure bitter cold or uncomfortably hot weather, it is better than to live in hell.

Chapter Eighteen: Great Teamwork
(Speaking About Service, Duty and Gratitude)

O ur lives are short, but the universe exists forever. Although we present new things that are etched into human history, our basic needs such as food, clothing and love have remain unchanged.

T hose who live to help others are not afraid of the hardships standing before them. These people are willing to shoulder the heaviest of responsibilities when helping others, even if only a little of the world's pain is relieved by their efforts. They do not seek any reward; they are merely motivated by a kind heart.

e should cultivate a spirit of independence. Do not rely on others for help. There is nothing impossible when we are confident.

 gentleman will do the best he can to fulfill his duty. He does not care about how much time he has to spend on his work; he only wants to do it well.

 ife is worth living when you are given great responsibility. Life will be empty and meaningless when one evades one's responsibilities.

 man is more admirable when he is strong and brave enough to take the responsibility for a difficult task.

Do not try to do the easy jobs all the time. You miss the chance of becoming strong and experienced by doing so. You will be given a great responsibility only when you prove your worth by doing difficult work.

You will have a peaceful mind when your life is ordinary and quiet, because you will not worry about gains or losses in life.

No one is an island in the modern world. Thus, we should be grateful to those who make our survival possible. Be generous, since you have reached what you have through the help of others in society.

Be grateful to those who receive your help, since in turn they give you a chance to make meritorious contributions, as would a Bodhisattva. These opportunities demonstrate the fact that life is filled with changes. How, then, can we afford to ignore any chance for helping others when we are healthy and have money to spare?

To remove our worldly desires is not enough; we need to have a heart of gratitude. We must not expect the recipients of our charity to give us thanks. We should thank them for giving us the opportunity to show our good character of generosity. Be grateful to those who are in need of help, since through helping them we can see our own kindness.

Chapter Nineteen: A Spiritual Antibody

(*Speaking About Confidence, Perseverance and Courage*)

Be persistent in the midst of adversity and distress. Do not stray from your goal in life when others try to lure you away.

Nothing is impossible, if we have courage and confidence. The only obstacle to your success is when you tell yourself, "I do not want to."

We can demonstrate the spirit of perseverance through working hard. We need this attitude in order to achieve something great.

A Spiritual Antibody

Taiwan has become more prosperous and democratic. Thus, we should now strive to strengthen our spiritual lives in order to purify our minds.

We must have confidence, perseverance and moral courage so that we will not be dominated or manipulated by other people. This is like to be strengthened by taking a spiritual antibody. Once we take it in, we become immune to worldly temptations.

Our spiritual lives are very important. We can live happily if we are rich spiritually, even if we are materially poor.

The work we must complete is like a road. No matter how far the road extends and how tired we are, we should try our best to complete the journey. This is a demonstration of the spirit of persever-

97

ance.

 We must cultivate a strong confidence if we want to imitate Buddha's behavior. We should also have the courage to remove worries and worldly desires, so that we can live happily and freely.

If we do not trust ourselves, we will become lost along life's voyage, and thus grow degenerate. If we are suspicious, we will not be able to establish good relations with other people. Consequently, it will be difficult to accomplish anything meaningful.

Some people idle away their lives and, thus, accomplish nothing. The major reason for this is their lack of confidence and courage for facing reality. Weak people are especially vulnerable to human events.

Believing in Buddha will not give you fame and money. It will simply make you feel confident and brave, so that you will not always rely on other people. Therefore, we should set a good example for others by behaving properly, receiving Buddha's teachings carefully, and making a contribution to society.

You will be as wise as a Bodhisattva if you can make an inhumane person merciful, a jealous one tolerant, a stingy one generous, an evil one kind. To do so is a meritorious deed, and you also make yourself as noble as Buddha himself.

Chapter Twenty: We Should Often Draw the Well Water
(*Speaking About Luck, Fortune and Happiness*)

T here are four ways to acquire good Karma (fate). They are to unremittingly carry out Buddha's teachings, be merciful, enlighten fellow humans, and calmly tolerate insults.

W e should love other people in order to receive a plenitude of good fortune. The more you reach out to help and to love, the more good fortune you will obtain. It is always better to offer help than to seek help.

I   t is a good idea to cultivate insight if becoming wealthy. To gain both good fortune and insight, we must extend our love to everyone in society by sharing our time and money.

U   nselfish giving will make us happy and relaxed. The donor will become delighted and happy, while the recipient will enjoy material support and feel warmth and love spiritually.

L   uck can keep a person away from disaster and trouble. A lucky person can handle unfavorable episodes successfully. Luck is a form of good fortune.

W   ealth does not always guarantee good fortune. True good fortune means peacefulness.

STILL THOUGHTS

The four boundless states of mind include the love of others, compassion, sympathetic joy (to be glad when fortune comes to others) and unselfish giving. They are at the core of Buddhism. The reason Buddha trains us through various methods is to help us let go of earthly desires and unworthy cares.

Life is filled with changes, and it is hard to maintain the integrity of a nation forever. We should not be too critical or concerned when we are alive. It is, in fact, a great fortune if we have a peaceful mind that enables us to do what we want for having a good time.

We will receive greater fortune if we become forgiving and thoughtful. That is why Buddhists say, "It is a good fortune to be forgiving."

When we draw well water, the water table will never fall. To give unselfishly is equivalent to drawing well water; no matter how much water you draw, the water level remains the same. The more you contribute, the more you gain. A well's water table is not going to rise if you do not draw water from it.

We should utilize our time, and develop the functions of our lives in order to help all living beings. The more we give unselfishly to others, the more we realize that life is meaningful and significant. We can thus live a happy life.

Each of us aspires to live happily, but happiness is something that cannot be measured by material possessions. It is a feeling. We can enjoy our lives if we feel content mentally. A person with a content mind is definitely broad-minded and, consequently, he is tolerant and kind to others.

STILL THOUGHTS

Disease is something unbearable and there is nothing we can do. There is a Chinese saying that goes, "Even a big hero turns into a lamb when he is sick." A healthy body is the greatest fortune that one can have, and it is useless to give a sick man a lot of money or power. We can be happy only if we live in good health.

It is a good idea to wish ourselves and, above all, our children good luck. We should always do the best we can to help others. Do not underestimate each individual's efforts; if we pool all of our effort we can help a lot of people. Regardless of our social status, each person's meritorious deed is equally valuable.

Chapter Twenty-One: Spiritual Relief
(*Speaking About Mercy and Wisdom*)

Be merciful. Try to regard the unhappiness and pains of others as your own. Then, you will be qualified to join the work of helping others.

We can achieve true spiritual relief by learning the Buddha's wisdom in order to develop the four boundless states of mind, including the love of others, compassion, sympathetic joy and unselfish giving. Then, we can live happily and appreciate the significance of life.

STILL THOUGHTS

I hope we can spread love and mercy to all living beings in every corner of the world. Let them be as happy as if they are bathing in the delightful moonlight.

A merciful man will behave gently. Mercy and gentleness can help a person eliminate his worries.

D o not look down on yourself. Every living being is as wise and merciful as Buddha. Whatever Buddha can do, you can do.

T he core of mercy is love and benevolence. We must offer our mercy to others with sincerity and kindness.

T ry to develop Buddha's state of mind as your own state of mind, and try to regard your Dharma Master's spiritual career as your own. The

Buddha's state of mind envelopes the four boundless states of mind: the love of others, compassion, sympathetic joy and unselfish giving. As well, the master's spiritual career includes charity, medicine, education and culture.

T he love of others and sympathetic joy mean to spread and share your happiness with people living around you. Compassion means to immediately save living beings that are in trouble. Unselfish giving means to teach others all you know without holding back.

W e must be free from the bondage of delusion, if we want to play our role wisely on the stage of life. A man will become evil if he is dominated by the delusion of lust. We should, therefore, rid ourselves of delusion by lighting up the lamp of wisdom in our hearts. If we can broaden our range of passion, it will yield a love as pure as the Bodhisattva's.

STILL THOUGHTS

To grow more intellectual is not the purpose for studying Buddhist sutras. We study sutras to become inspired by Buddha's wisdom. The source of wisdom comes from concentration of mind and from reasonable behavior.

"Prajna" means supreme wisdom. We have to use wisdom to choose our friends and professions. We cannot accomplish anything great without wise selection. We will acquire the Buddha's wisdom of complete relief if we regard deep meditation as our father and Prajna as our mother.

What does wisdom mean? It stands for kindness. A kind man knows how to appreciate things that make others happy, and he does things that benefit others. If a man only does things that benefit himself, he is only a smart, not a wise, man.

We should offer our pure love even to people with whom we do not have a special relationship, and we should have the compassion to share in the unhappiness of others. This is the fundamental spirit of a Buddhist. There is no need for Buddhism if the substance of mercy is extracted from it.

A true life of wisdom is based on a sincere and humble manner like that of a Bodhisattva's. We should talk gently and behave kindly, so that people around us can sense our warmth and happiness.

Even an intelligent man can become bothered with all kinds of problems. He should wash away the dirt of the problems with the water of wisdom, so that he can maintain a clear mind.

Chapter Twenty-Two: To Sprinkle a Drop of Sweet Dew

(Less Desire and More Contentment)

D o not worry that you may be less capable than others. Try to be helpful and kind to others. This is the formula for a happy life.

T here is little difference between an dissatisfied man and an unwise man. We are the masters of the things we possess, not the other way around.

To beg for something is always painful. If we keep begging others we will gain nothing but countless disturbances.

Mankind's worldly desires are like a hot and dry desert. But Buddha's teachings are like sweet dew; they quench our thirst and cleanse away unnecessary desires.

If we can reduce our desire, then all worries that bother us will disappear.

Less desire and more contentment. It is the prerequisite for learning Buddha's wisdom so you can achieve a peaceful heart and wise mind.

When a person always dresses plainly and neatly, and keeps himself well-groomed, we can conclude that he lives a promising life. Contrarily,

111

when a person likes to show off his luxurious new clothes, we can surmise that he is being occupied by countless desires of vanity.

S ome people's desires can never be satisfied. When they have money and fame they ask for more. If a person feels content with what he has, he is surely a happy man. It is impossible to own all the world's valuables. A person will only create trouble for himself if he keeps chasing material wealth and lustful enjoyment. Contentment is the only solution for terminating his endless desires.

C ontentment will make one's life happy and peaceful. A content man finds comfort in any place, whereas a discontent man complains even in paradise.

T here is little difference between a discontent, wealthy man and a poor man. A content, poor person may be deficient materially, but he can be wealthy spiritually.

A content man will not hesitate to love others and do his share of good deeds, no matter how limited he is. A loving person is always a content person, and a content person is always a wealthy person. Wealth and fortune are not only something that can be counted with money.

A man should be content and happy with what he has. Be thrifty, so that you can have spare money to share with others. We should devote what we have -- money and time -- to the poor who are in need of our help. Doing so is known as performing the countless meritorious deeds.

STILL THOUGHTS

T he relaxing smile of a patient, or anyone else who has received much-needed help, is like the warm sunshine after a thunderstorm. It comforts those around him -- his relatives, friends, doctors and nurses.

Chapter Twenty-Three: Mastery Comes From Training
(Speaking About the Ego-Center)

W e cannot ask others to make possible something that is impossible. But we should demand this level of accomplishment of ourselves.

W e should strive to be as smooth and polished as a sea-washed pebble, rather than acting like the rough, uncut stones dynamited from mountain-side cliffs.

STILL THOUGHTS

Even though you may feign stupidity toward others, you can never trick yourself. Trying to do so wastes your time and your life.

Do not look down on small contributions to society as being shabby. Even the tiniest bolt must be screwed on tightly.

Do not assume that you are more important than others. Egotism is a source of trouble and ailment. Look upon yourself lightly, as if you did not exist in the world.

Before requiring that others act perfectly, you must first require that of yourself. Accommodate others while not demanding that they accommodate you.

I f we want to truly help others eliminate their troubles, we must do so wisely according to what they really need.

P eople often forget the meaning of humility. They behave arrogantly after learning but a little. They think and talk always of themselves. Such opinionated egotists are intractable. Their hearts are full of arrogance.

P ut yourself under scrutiny. Ask: Where was I before I was born? Who am I? What did I really gain after arguing with others today? At which moment did I show my true self to others? By gazing inward, you will probably discover that each of us is but an illusion.

T he way that a man talks reveals his character and credibility. He must cultivate a strong moral character to make himself trustworthy. *117*

STILL THOUGHTS

He can cultivate his moral character by behaving sincerely, honestly, and refraining from criticizing others behind their backs.

A ccepting the criticism of others is a type of moral lesson. You should listen carefully and re-examine your conscience. You should eliminate the negative qualities of arrogance, stubbornness and egotism, so that you can cultivate morality for behaving properly.

I n order to forge a piece of pig iron into a useful tool, we must melt and refine it in a furnace, and then hammer and bend it into the proper shape. The scoldings we receive from others are like the hot fire in a furnace. If we can bear these trials, we will become shaped into useful people. Do not forget that a successful man must endure all sorts of tests.

We should constantly re-examine our behavior; we may have good intentions in mind, but are we actually putting them into practice? Consider how your words and actions may have offended others. Through constant self-examination we avoid making big mistakes.

People's minds often change according to the influences of the outside world. We hold our heads high when we are in favorable circumstances, only to grieve and weep when facing troubles. A man's mind cannot remain calm if his emotions are dominated by the outside world.

Chapter Twenty-Four: We Come and Go Empty-Handed.
(*Speaking About Letting It Go*)

Accomplishing countless meritorious deeds is equivalent to eradicating countless griefs. By doing so, one not only sails across the river of distress, but also reaches the goal of spiritual delivery.

We should frequently wish ourselves luck for accomplishing our endeavors, relax, and be happy.

As members of society, we cannot expect to get away from worldly affairs. A person is in tune with worldly affairs if he maintains a good interrelationship with others, has an open mind and optimistic personality, and performs his duties well.

We can say that a person has a good perception of the essence of wisdom if he is capable of obtaining Prajna (the supreme wisdom) by clearly understanding every truth that Buddha teaches, and if he can remain calm in the midst of life's vicissitudes.

A person has a good perception of the essence of harmony if he can bring worldly affairs and wisdom into balance while refusing to be restrained by these two.

In order to cultivate mercy and delight in our hearts, we must forget all the worries that bothered us just a minute ago.

STILL THOUGHTS

I f we want to free our minds from ideological bondage and have a profound understanding of life and death, we must cultivate the idea of "letting go."

Chapter Twenty-Five: The Enormous Power of Compassion
(*Speaking About the Spiritual Careers of the Tzu Chi Association*)

We should be constantly concerned about the Tzu Chi Association, and be brave and happy when we face challenges and difficulties. We should make the most of our lives, and combine all our resources to do things that benefit living beings.

All the commissioners of Tzu Chi have hearts as compassionate as a Bodhisattva's. They serve as the hands and eyes of the "one-thousand-hand and one-thousand-eye" Goddess of Mercy. Through these commissioners, we can see the enormous power of compas-

123

sion.

T here are several prerequisites for voluntary workers in the Tzu Chi Hospital: One must endure hardship and work diligently.

T he busier, the happier. It is important to realize that the more you do, the more energetic you will be. Be gentle and relaxed. Consider this example: You should be calm when trying to cheer up a cancer victim. Do not exhibit a lamentable attitude.

T hose who are blessed by Buddha can easily come by riches. For them, riches can be earned within seconds. However, other people are not so fortunate. They can hardly save any money, even though they are constantly running around like headless chickens. The Tzu Chi Association is like a fertile rice paddy. You plant in it the seeds of good fortune, and you reap from it a fine harvest at the time of your reincarnation.

T he Tzu Chi Commissioners must maintain a charming demeanor and an immaculate appearance. They must wear the spirit of Buddhism on their right shoulder, the good image of Tzu Chi on their left, and present a warm personality that comes directly from the heart.

T hose who participate in the activities of the Tzu Chi Association must be equipped with the spirit of a loyal volunteer. They must help and encourage one another. Do not become paranoid when you are in trouble. If you compare yourself with others objectively, you may fall short of the best, but you will be better than the worst. Be sure to make resolutions that are beneficial to others.

D oing the work of Tzu Chi is like pushing a cart uphill. We should perform it in one determined breath. The cart will surely slide downhill if we stop our task halfway.

People who take part in Tzu Chi activities aim to touch the conscience of the general public; one more Tzu Chi advocate means one less troubled soul.

The reason why social customs are growing worse is because so many people lust for extravagant lifestyles. They become dreamy-eyed and unrealistic. We want to change lifestyles of this sort into ones of simplicity and sincerity by inviting these people to take part in Tzu Chi activities. Their families will be happier, and our society more peaceful, if we guide them toward doing something meaningful to make the most of their leisure time.

Karma (or "fated opportunity") fulfills all kinds of charitable careers. However, these careers can only be accomplished if we grasp the arrival of Karma. The vast Tzu Chi family is the right place for us to fulfill our hope of helping others to act as a Bodhisattva.

I t is wiser to look upon society with confidence and love, rather than from a perspective of worry.

I f we want to accomplish the spiritual career as espoused by Buddha, we must endure numerous tests and trials. If we want to create a sharp knife, we must hammer and forge it. In the same way, we must do what is necessary in order to join the Tzu Chi and accomplish the spiritual career espoused by Buddha. We should never quit when facing difficulties.

Chapter Twenty-Six: Drinking the Water of the Glass of Wisdom

(*Speaking About Delivery, Impermanence and Rapid Progress*)

Delivery means to use mercy as a way for saving and helping others.

The wisdom of Buddha's philosophy is suitable for people of all educational backgrounds. For those who have received higher education, Buddha's philosophy is profound and penetrating. For people who have achieved the academic norm, Buddha's philosophy proves to be very useful. For those who have received little formal education, Buddha's philosophy is something they can truly count on.

The reason why we repeatedly chant Buddha's name for people who are preparing for reincarnation is to make them less frightened so they can achieve rebirth peacefully. But chanting Buddha's name does not guarantee that the people who are about to die will make a trip to the Western World (or "Paradise"). If there were such a guarantee, we would not need to cultivate virtue or believe in the concept of cause and effect.

We take the seven-day Buddhist lessons in order to know how to worship Buddha properly, and to understand Buddhist manner and rules. We should listen carefully to the lectures on Buddha's philosophy, and bear in mind that wisdom. It is of great help to purify our bodies, minds and words through the seven-day contemplation lessons.

STILL THOUGHTS

If we want to preach Buddha's philosophy, we must do so with perseverance. If a man is invested with the spirit of perseverance, he will be immune to agony, worry and negligence. Eventually, he will gain wisdom.

How can we create good fortune? We must first learn to cherish good fortune and create it for others, then ultimately we will be able to harvest from the three kinds of "paddies of great fortune." Nourishment from the paddy of gratitude helps us fulfill our filial obligations and honor our teachers. The paddy of respect helps us revere Buddha, his philosophy and his disciples. The paddy of mercy assists us to look after patients, help the poor and be merciful to all beings.

The Sutra of Medicine, which sets forth much of Buddha's wisdom, aims to console people who are suffering from physical or mental disabilities. Buddha opens the door to enlightenment for healthy and unhealthy people alike.

The Karma force is invisible, and it is generated by our behavior in the past. People are born to the same race and nation because they possess a similar Karma force. However, each individual's Karma has unique characteristics. Your Karma force dictates your features, family, and whether you will be rich or poor, wise or naive.

When a person speaks a lot of nothing, we say that he is just playing with words. An articulate man can deliver a long speech in front of a crowd, but what he says may have no significance for daily life. He is simply playing with words. The same is true when a man studies Buddha's philosophy, yet fails to put it into practice.

Life and death are both impermanent. People often become confused, regarding impermanence as permanence, and unhappiness as happiness. Usually, their minds became distorted due to something unwholesome they did. People tend to get lost on life's voyage.

One can make rapid progress by restricting himself and constantly re-examining his behavior. It is also important to make one's self presentable to others.

If you have confidence, you can sail across any river, though it may be wide. But if you lack confidence, it is impossible for you to cross even the narrowest creek.

Many Buddhists go on pilgrimages to the mountains, which they respect as symbols of virtue. Along the way, these Buddhist pilgrims prostrate themselves every three steps. In doing so, they are able to become enlightened by the sense of morality that exists deep in their hearts. An old Chinese poem goes as follows: You need not search long for Buddha's Spirit Mountain; It exists no where else but in your heart; Everyone has a pagoda on Spirit Mountain where he can go to cultivate virtue. It is a true form of virtue-cultivation when we bring the spirit of pilgrimage into our daily conduct.

Chapter Twenty-Seven: Let Everyone Have a Smiling Face
(Abstaining From Slaughter)

A ltruism is an ideal we must fulfill according to the needs and requests of others. At the core of altruism is mercy. Also, the focus of Buddha's philosophy is on one's genuine character. Thus, it is difficult for a person to achieve enlightenment, if while he abides by the rule of supreme calmness he chooses to ignore the events happening around him. If we really want our actions to benefit others, we must act according to the hopes and needs of those around us. In the same way, we must behave like a Bodhisattva before we can become as good as a Buddha.

We can best appreciate the beauty of nature on a chilly winter day when the plum trees are in full bloom. Only when we offer our love and concern to those in trouble, can we say to them that life is not cruel.

Let us warm the sorrowful hearts of others with our sincerity and eagerness for helping.

A family's poverty and unhappiness is generally caused by illness. Thus, it is possible for us to help revitalize the family's well-being by teaching its members to take precautions against disease, and by curing the sick members so they can stand up to help shoulder family responsibilities.

STILL THOUGHTS

A healthy, productive society must be based on the concept of mutual help. People sometimes unwittingly ruin the good image of others. This act can be compared to throwing a handful of dust into the wind, a gesture that only soils your own face. You can never slander others without damaging your own reputation.

I t is a showing of benevolence if you refuse to slaughter any living creature. Benevolence is a kind of love. All philosophies and forms of truth are based on love. Love prevents us from killing and enables us to protect all living beings. As humans, we are capable of sensing sorrow and pain. We should put ourselves in the position of others, so that we can better sympathize with all that suffer from poverty, illness and distress. Give alms to the poor. Send the sick to a hospital. Try to encourage others to do the same. These acts are the best ways to protect lives.

I t is a bad idea to set domesticated animals that depend on us free into the wilds. To do so is to release them to a certain death. It is better to provide assistance to those in need, than to release the caged unattended into the wilds.

Chapter Twenty-Eight: Life Is Short
(*How to Live a Fruitful Life*)

O ur lives are sustained by our breaths, and we never know when they will cease. Every second is of vital importance. Our lives, in fact, are measured in seconds, and not in years. By realizing this, we can better appreciate our lives. Those who cherish good fortune are definitely those who do good things for others. Those who do good things for others are definitely happy people. Each of us can enjoy a fruitful life by always being happy.

I ndeed, how swiftly time passes. An opportunity for learning slips through one's fingers only too easily. Grasp the chance, or you will regret not doing so when you are old.

A person will waste his time if he dose nothing but groan about his troubles and pains. What makes the matter worse, is that all his troubles and pains double when he acts in such a manner.

W e are able to carry our studies, professions and spiritual careers to completion when we use time properly. Our meritorious deeds are accumulated continuously, day after day, throughout our lives. To a wise man, time is a diamond. But to a fool, it is a lump of dirt. Therefore, nothing is impossible, if we cherish our time as if it was a diamond, and concentrate our minds on pursuing good deeds. However, we accomplish nothing, and even become a burden to society, if we waste our time heedlessly.

STILL THOUGHTS

We live in the world only for a few decades. As such, each day's conduct is more significant than the span of our brief lives. All our daily actions are accumulated to compose the whole of our lives. Our behavior each day determines whether our lives end up being meaningful or meaningless.

When a person becomes bogged down in the pursuit of wealth, he forfeits the right to use that wealth, and is thus deprived of the noble character needed to reach out and help others. Eventually, he becomes isolated or even forgotten by society. His life grows more lonely and miserable than that of a poor man.

The poor suffer from a deficiency of material goods, yet the rich lack the fulfillment of a spiritual life. The poor try everything they can to obtain luxury items they do not possess. The rich, on the other hand, are afraid of losing what they have, and this is why they do not live happily.

Some of the poor are also poor spiritually. These people are ignorant and narrow-minded. Moreover, upon becoming sick they drift away to become distant and isolated. They often die without notice.

There is yet another group of people who are materially poor, but spiritually rich. Though destitute, they have warm hearts that encourage them to love. They welcome you with smiling faces, and talk to you as a friend. Their lives are happy and rich in content.

Chapter Twenty-Nine: Our Hearts Are the Dwellings for Studying Buddhist Philosophy
(How to Get Along With Others and Deal With Problems)

I f we want to accomplish something great, we need to summon the participation of all our resources. When we are upset by something, we should remove our prejudices toward others.

W hen dealing with problems, we should act rationally and not purely on emotion. But when we endeavor to get along well with others, it is just the other way around; emotion becomes more important than rationality. In this way, we make ourselves popular and conduct our business efficiently.

"An upright heart is the correct dwelling wherein we can study Buddhist philosophy." An upright heart is one of honesty and probity, and it is the fundamental element for determining all our conduct. Be honest in dealing with people. We should never deceive ourselves or others. We should always remember that an upright heart is the proper dwelling for studying Buddhist philosophy. By maintaining this posture, we become a good disciple of Buddha, and behave as he did.

When dealing with people, we should set a good example in the way we behave. Be aware of your words, manner and intentions, so that you will be respected and respectful.

"It is hard to be a loving person and it is hard to do things that benefit others," some people often say. It is indeed difficult to behave properly. A person can become evil, greedy and corrupt just as

143

soon as one bad idea crosses his mind. If we scrutinize our society to find its fundamental problem, we will discover that most of us have lost the noble character of one who loves and cares.

Part 2

Questions &

Answers

(Compiled by Master Cheng Yen's Disciples)

Section One: Human Affairs
Speaking About Love

A member of the Tzu Chi Association who engages in the fields of culture and education suffered the loss of her beloved husband. She then went to see the Master.

The Master consoled her with: "Don't count a man's life by his age; it should be counted by his achievements. Your husband made enormous contributions to his family and work. If you truly miss him, you should carry on his spirit of dedication, and demonstrate your own talents as well. You should devote your time and energy to educating your children, purifying our society, and promoting our traditional virtues and culture.

"Don't confine yourself only to your family," the Master continued, "and do not become depressed simply because you lost your husband's support. Chin up, chest out! Be confident. You should extend your love and concern to other people, and develop the function of your life to the utmost."

"I will try it gradually... " the member replied.

"You should do it immediately," the Master interjected. "Life is filled with changes. We must seize the day. Someone asked me, 'Do you have any plans for the future, Master?' I said I certainly have plans and goals for the future, yet I must live for the moment. Our achievements in the future are based on our daily endeavors. The future is an accumulation of many 'todays.' Consider that well."

"I haven't been able to calm down during the last three months," the member confided. "I locked myself in my office, and didn't want to face others or join any meetings. This situation continued until I dreamed of my husband telling me that he would not be able to come back.

147

STILL THOUGHTS

Suddenly, Master, I understood what you meant by your words, 'You should stop missing him all the time.'"

The Master elaborated: "Your husband is physically free from all worldly worries. Do not drag him down. It is your own problem if you cannot let him go. Life is like a play, and each of us has a different role on the stage. Some play major roles, some minor roles. The major role players must continue to perform when the minor role players come down from the stage. You have successfully played the different roles of a wife, mother and good daughter-in-law. From now on, you have a new role to play -- that of a Bodhisattva. You must improve your knowledge and become a good teacher and helpful friend for your students. Teach all you know to your students, and to others, without holding back. Education is a work filled with great enjoyment and unselfish giving. A true educator will teach people how to obtain spiritual enjoyment. We will never enjoy a fulfilling life if we are rich materially but deficient spiritually. The promoting of culture is aimed at purifying our hearts so that we can appreciate the significance of life and cherish our good fortune. People can then live happily and peacefully. That is why education is a work filled with great enjoyment.

"The education of the people takes a hundred years to bear fruit. Be sure to devote your time and wisdom to your students and teach them all you know. That is what I call unselfish giving. Buddha's heart is filled with mercy, and a Bodhisattva's heart is filled with great enjoyment and the virtue of unselfish giving. What concerns a Bodhisattva most is the plight of the poor and pitiable beings. You should develop the function of life and be helpful to others.

"The Sutra of the Heart says, 'Thou shall not worry. When there is no worry, there is no fear. Thou shall then be kept away from confusion and delusion.' Do not worry to excess.

"Life is like a drama with a Bodhisattva playing all sorts of roles on the stage. Hope that you can successfully and happily perform another role in the new play."

STILL THOUGHTS

O ne member complained: "I recently found out that while I was living abroad the past few years my husband betrayed me by having an affair with one of my best friends. Now, he has since died, yet I remain angry."

"You should not be angry with a person who has already passed away," the Master replied.

"I am not angry with dead one," the member explained. "I am angry with the one that is still alive."

The Master responded: "You must not look back on things that have already happened. Live only for today. We should live as if we were walking along a tightrope. You will fall if you keep looking back rather than forward. You should have forgiven him and shown love to the one he loved while he was still alive. What will you gain if you complain to others after he has gone?"

M any people's complaints are related to family disputes. They wonder why love is filled with uncertainty.

Considering this, the Master said: "Lovers are always making a solemn pledge of everlasting love before getting married. However, their relationship sours once the honeymoon is over. It is silly of some people to commit suicide due to being deserted by their lovers.

Do we only live in the pursuit of this kind of love? It is an evil act to destroy the body, which was given to us by our parents, simply because we are no longer loved by someone. We should understand the rule of carefully looking after our physical forms, since our bodies were given to us by our parents."

A member complained, "Master, my husband doesn't want to take care of the family. It is I who suffers the burden of looking after the 17 people in our household. I can hardly bear it any longer."

"His family is also your family," The Master replied. "Your husband does so because he knows you are very capable. You are not tolerant enough, if you regard the responsibility as suffering. It is true you have to look after

17 people. But remember that I must look after even more people. On the one hand, I must pray for hundreds of thousands of kind people, wishing their families good luck. I must assume the responsibility of educating the rich to the importance of planting the seeds of mercy and kindness in society. They can reap good fortune for themselves by performing kind and meritorious deeds for others. On the other hand, I also need to perform many charitable activities, such as the monthly relief for the poor program and raising special financial aid in the case of sudden emergencies. I, too, face many difficulties in dealing with so many people and projects. But I'm willing to do my work without complaint, despite the hardships and criticisms, so long as I can help all living beings."

One member's husband is very obedient to her in many ways, but she is still unhappy. "Master," she said, "he is sometimes unfaithful. It is unfortunate, and pains me so. What should I do?"

The Master replied: "Do not be too pushy. Love is like

a ball; the harder you throw it against the ground, the higher it will bounce. Do not strangle your husband with excessive love. If you do so, he will politely keep you at arm's distance. Be gentle and thoughtful to him, and not possessive. If you give him too much pressure, he will be obedient to you only in appearance. In fact, he is probably afraid of you in his heart. No wonder he commits acts of unfaithfulness. Try to extend your love to the one he loves. When he realizes what you are doing, he will feel grateful toward you. He will then cherish your love more deeply, realizing that you are providing space for him to grow and breathe. Our emotions are sometimes like a furnace; no matter how cold his heart may be, you can warm it with your sincere love."

A member's husband always takes home his troubles and frustrations. What is worse, he likes to take them out on her. She is bothered by this constantly.

The Master told her: "A husband's psychological problem can only be healed by his wife. Be sure to encourage him and show your love to him."

"Yes, this I do," she replied. "Whenever he complains to me, I say, 'Take it easy. Life is this way.'"

The Master said: "It is you who are wrong. The next time, you should tell him, 'I understand how painful you feel. You have suffered much for me and our children. I appreciate very much all your endeavors.'"

A certain member of the Tzu Chi Association is very much concerned about his children's marriages, a situation upon which the Master expounded: "Parents give physical birth to their children, but they cannot give them a spiritual life or good fortune. Each person has his own fated opportunity and destiny. If we are determined to imitate a Bodhisattva's behavior, we must make a strong resolution to extend our love to all living beings for the rest of our lives. All parents should acknowledge the fact that they bear responsibility for their children, but do not exercise rights over them."

All my children are adults now, but I still doubt that they can take care of themselves. It troubles me," the member said.

The Master responded: "You must let go. Your extreme concern for your children will cause you nothing but vexation. Your children can take care of themselves because they have grown up. Our lives are filled with changes and uncertainty. You should grasp every chance to perform meritorious deeds."

Another member said: "I know it is against Buddha's philosophy to hate others. Even so, I can't help but hate my husband, since he is having an extra-marital affair."

To this the Master said: "It is so difficult for the ordinary person to distinguish between true love and infatuation. You should love the one your husband loves. Try to change his infatuation for another into a form of pure love for you, like that of a Bodhisattva's love. Religious faith is

155

more than only taking part in religious rituals. You must understand the Bodhisattva of the Earth Treasury's great spirit of mercy instead of only chanting his name all the time. Your husband and mother-in-law are just the right persons for you to show your love and concern to."

"If I make a resolution to do good things for others, will it help improve my son's Karma?" a member asked.

The Master answered with: "It is our duty to do good things, and it will certainly bring good fortune to you if you make a resolution to do things that benefit others. We should bravely face the challenges that are destined to happen in our lives. Our Karma, whether it is good or bad, can always serve as a warning to us; it is set down according to our behavior. We should never ask for anything we do not deserve to have."

How can a housewife become a good Buddhist? To this question, the Master responded: "Our existence in the world is highly significant. As a human being, you should abide by the rules of society. Only when a housewife fulfills a housewife's duty, will she qualify to become a Buddhist. A good housewife's contributions to her family and society are enormous. In fact, she has three different roles to play in order to become a good Buddhist:

"She must be a good daughter-in-law. She needs to embrace the concept of filial piety by serving her father- and mother-in-law well. It is always wiser to respect the two living Buddhas at home, rather than to worship a stone Buddha in a temple; She must be a good wife. She should look after her husband, and help society sweep away pornographic businesses. She should also encourage her husband to devote his efforts to his spiritual career; and she must be a good mother. She should increase her knowledge in every field, so that she can become a good teacher and mentor for her children. She should make sure that her children are healthy and strong, both physically and mentally."

A disciple of the Master said: "Every family has some sort of problem."

The Master replied: "Knowing that fact, you should always remain calm."

The member elaborated: "I'm worried about my son. He is 36 years old, and still single."

The Master said: "Don't be pushy. You must let nature take its course. Otherwise, you might become regretful in the future."

My son is addicted to playing video games," another member complained. "I tell him not to waste his time on such things, but he always turns a deaf ear. This bothers me very much."

To this the Master replied: "One can hardly control a man of 28.

"He will stop when he is tired of playing. As we often say, 'He will be bored with the game when it is out of fashion.' Do not nag him.

"Simply remind him now and then."

A visitor asked: "I have listened to a tape of one of your lectures. I feel that we should begin to improve the educational environment in our families, but I don't know how."

"You don't need to hold any special activity," the Master explained. "Just try to encourage all parents to extend their love to the schoolchildren of others. Do not restrict your love to your own children. If you keep blowing on the same balloon, it will explode before long. You should love all living beings, and teach your children through Bodhisattva's wisdom."

A member asked: "My family is wealthy. However, my only son treats me as if I were his enemy."

The Master answered: "The Karma was sometimes created in the previous life. You can do nothing but face it when it comes. Try to be nice to him, and wish him good luck. At the moment we enter Paradise we can bring nothing with us but the Karma, no matter if it is good or bad. There are many examples for demonstrating that the wealth of a family does not bring happiness to its children. In fact, wealth sometimes creates a lot of headaches. Fortune can mean good luck and bad luck for a person. It all depends on the way you use it."

 member said: "My daughter's fiance is inferior to her in educational background and social status."

The Master's response was: "We should not be overly concerned about a person's fame. We cannot measure a person's wisdom by his diploma. Virtue is what really counts. We should plan to get married because of love, not because of fame or other such attractions."

A member confided: "I know that the one I love lied to me once, but I still love him. Whenever I see him, I feel like I want to punch his nose. But when he is away, I miss him dearly. I even want to die."

The Master responded: "Do not be so silly as to want to die for someone else. It is so easy to die; you should make your existence valuable. You can do a lot of great things for others. So why don't you? Our lives are short. That you have been ill-treated by someone is not something to be pitied. What is truly unfortunate is when you misuse your life."

M any parents fear that their children may not be able to pass the college entrance examination. To this the Master said: "The love between mother and child is great. However, it will disturb your child if he knows your concern is based on his exam performance. You should instead calm your worries by chanting Buddha's sutras. We are always gaining something and losing something. Besides, anyone can become a master in his field."

My husband scolded my son by saying, 'You will never make it unless the sky and earth change,'" a member said.

To this concern the Master answered: "The scolding was actually a blessing. The sky and earth are changing all the time; sometimes it is hot and sunny, when other times it becomes cold and cloudy. Your son will be very successful. Try to be understanding, for doing so will make you luckier and wiser."

Another member asked: "How can a professional woman take care of her family and career at the same time?"

"One of the best things for a woman to have is the glory of maternal instinct," the Master answered. "It is good for a professional woman to increase her knowledge by having a career, but she should not extinguish the glory of maternal instinct."

Sad and angry parents came to see the Master, depicting how their son was killed in a dispute.

The Master consoled them by saying: "Reprisal breeds reprisal.

"You would do better by forgetting. Try to forgive those who killed your son. By doing so, you can create more good fortune for your son. You should also chant Buddha's name on behalf of your son, so that he can be freed from the Karma. Do not be unduly remorseful. You should understand that physical birth is the start of death, and that death is the beginning of new life. Your son's death will help you understand the significance of life. Try to love other children who badly need your affection and concern. Your son will then be blessed."

One member said: "My wife had a heart attack because of offensive remarks by my son."

The Master responded: "There are proper

ways to educate our children. Be sure to encourage and praise them when they do things well, and remind them with few words when they behave badly. Timing is also very important when you want to correct their behavior. Times have changed. Your methods of educating your children should be improved just as your children improve their knowledge everyday."

A member said: "Our society has changed a lot. This has caused changes in the interrelationship of people, and also increased marital problems. How can a victim of societal change cope with the pain of an extra-marital affair?"

The Master answered: "Don't call it an affair. You should view it as a fated opportunity? It is part of your Karma. You should accept it bravely. You should keep loving and thanking your husband.

"He has given you a chance to see that our lives are filled with changes. You can grasp this chance to re-examine your conscience and readjust yourself. Do not see it as a form of hurting. It is a sin if you commit suicide, since you ruin the body given by your beloved parents. How can you eliminate the bad Karma when you do not have a body to carry out your goodwill. Both husband and wife should feel grateful if their marriage is pleasant. They should remain calm if their marriage is not as wonderful as they expected."

Speaking About Daughter and Mother-in-law

young woman who always talks back when being scolded by her mother-in-law went to see the Master in Hualien.

The Master said to her: "Your behavior was wrong. When your mother-in-law scolds you, you should not talk back."

This woman went home and did as the Master had said. When she met again with the Master, she said: "I did exactly what you taught me, but my mother-in-law became even more furious. She said I was turning a deaf ear to her. What should I do now?"

Speaking About Daughter and Mother-in-law

"How did you respond when she scolded you?" the Master asked.

"I just kept silent and turned a deaf ear to her," the woman replied.

The Master told her: "Again, you were wrong. When she is furious, you should behave obediently. When you throw a ball against the ground, it will bounce back. But when you throw a ball against a sponge, it does not bounce back. When she scolds you the next time, just smile to her and say, 'Yes, Mother. I understand and I will correct my fault.' If she is still mad at you, you should keep smiling and endure her angry words."

Later, the woman spoke with the Master in another location. "It worked," she said. "My mother-in-law doesn't scold me any more. She encourages me to listen to sutras, and she even helps me to do the dishes. I kept on smiling at her while she was scolding me. Finally, she started laughing along with me when she observed my smiling face."

STILL THOUGHTS

Another member said: "When my mother-in-law passed away, we were all living abroad together. Everything I arranged for in the funeral parlor was not in accordance with Chinese custom. Ever since then, I have been fighting with my brother- and sister-in-law, because they feel I was disrespectful to their mother."

The Master answered: "Let bygones be bygones. Otherwise, your mother-in-law cannot rest in peace."

A wealthy, elderly woman said: "Master, I don't want to give my money to my daughter-in-law in fear that she might misuse it. She is angry with me over this, even though I feel my intentions are good."

The Master replied: "Why don't you do as she wishes, since your intention is to help her? You should give your money to your daughter-in-law, so that she can learn the way of managing money. You will be freed from the burden of controlling money, and will win her gratitude. You are healthy now, but will you be able to manage money when you become sick? You had better put your daughter-in-law in charge of the family fortune. She will feel grateful to you, and thus will treat you nicer."

The woman met the Master a month later. "Thank you so much, Master. My life has become more enjoyable. First of all, I don't have to shoulder the burden of the family. Secondly, my daughter-in-law gives me NT$20,000 (about US$800) per month. It is enough for me to donate to charity. The interesting thing is that I did not dare donate that amount of money in the past in fear of exceeding the family budget."

Speaking About Illness

A terminal liver cancer patient became a convert of the Master.

The Master had told him: "A man's life can be divided in two: the filthy, mortal one, and the pure, eternal life of wisdom. A man should always be prepared to discard the filthy one when it becomes old and unable to be fixed, like a shabby house. We should grasp every chance to acquaint ourselves with Buddha's philosophy.

"We should also make the most of our limited lives in order to cultivate a kind heart like that of a Bodhisattva's. Do not forget that when the time comes for us to abandon the short, painful life, we still possess an eternal life of wisdom.

"A physical illness is not to be feared. What is really to be feared is when a man becomes ill spiritually. Cheer up and relax your eye brows. Life is short. We should live happily. An illness is not horrible; a patient simply needs to live at ease with it.

"It is proper for you to convert to Buddhism. But you must heed my advice -- stop worrying about life and death! A lot of patients become paranoid after finding out what illness they have. They go to see different doctors and take all sorts of medicine, only making matters worse. Yet when they decide to let go of all the treatments, they feel immeasurably better. Do not put pressure on yourself. Let nature take its course."

A member asked: "I have been imitating Buddha's behavior for years, and I understand Buddha's philosophy. But now I am sick. I feel fearful and don't know how to cope with it. What must I do to obtain the blessings of Buddha?"

The Master answered: "We do not receive the blessings of Buddha simply by aiming to imitate his behavior. As Buddhists, our aim is to cultivate courage. Buddha says, 'A man's Karma is irreversible.' The true essence of imitating Buddha's behavior lies in accepting our Karma fearlessly and calmly."

"Life is but a meaningless trip," exclaimed an elderly secular Buddhist devotee who, even though he cannot see clearly due to diabetes, chants sutras and worships Buddha everyday.

The Master replied: "This is not true. Your life's journey will not be a waste because you have learned Buddha's philosophy and wisdom."

Another elderly secular Buddhist devotee who is also of declining health said he believes his days are numbered. He hopes he will have a stronger body when he is reincarnated, so that he can help more people. But what bothers him is that he feels he might not become a Buddhist in his next life.

To him the Master said: "Let nature take its course. You will be able to help many people, if you can recover from your illness sooner. The people living around us, no matter how many of them there are, need our care and concern very much. If we cannot help deliver them from their troubles now, how can we expect to help them in the next life? No one can imitate Buddha's behavior when losing contact with the living beings. We should grasp every opportunity to spread Buddhist philosophy to the living while we ourselves are still alive.

"Do not treat yourself as a sick man. Try to relax and live actively, for time is precious. Your strong desire to live is important."

A member said: "Master, be sure to take good care of yourself."

The Master said: "No one is perfect. Each of us has some physical or mental trouble. One's physical illness is not to be regarded as horrible; it is only part of our bad Karma. I have suffered from various illnesses. However, my heart is peaceful. What really worries me are the obstacles lying ahead of me regarding the implementation of the four spiritual careers of the Tzu Chi Association.

"I would rather replace the obstacles with my own physical pains. The world is a world full of tolerance. We must have the spirit of tolerance while living in the world. Our bodies are but an appearance; I hope you can pay more attention to my life of wisdom."

A medical student expressed deep sorrow over the death of one of his close relatives.

The Master consoled him with: "Since you are a medical student, you will face many patients in the future. You should have a deep understanding of life and death. In Buddhism, death means a form of rebirth. The dead are leaving for a new life. Life and death are cyclical. Therefore, death is not sad. We should pray for the dead and chant sutras for them."

"What can I do for the reborn person?" the medical student continued.

The Master answered: "Be a good student. Study hard so that you can save a lot of patients in the future. Our bodies are given to us by our parents. The best way you can show your gratitude to them is to develop your life's function for helping others."

T o an elderly gentleman suffering from stomach cancer, the Master said: "Thirty percent of a man's illness is physical pain, while the remaining seventy percent is mental pain. A sick man needs to maintain a calm mentality. You need to release your anguish audibly, whether the sounds are groans of pain or joyous sutra chants. You must demonstrate your sorrow or happiness with facial expressions. You should be aware that your joyful sounds and happy facial expressions would bring comfort to others, as well as yourself."

STILL THOUGHTS

 member said: "I have been suffering from chest pain for years. I feel I only have a short time left, and my desire for living is growing weaker and weaker."

The Master responded: "You should rise and sleep according to a set schedule. Have a physical or see a doctor when necessary. Do not lose the strong will for struggling. You should let doctors take care of your body, while letting Bodhisattvas look after your mind and soul."

A visitor asked: "What is your opinion of life?"

The Master answered: "Our lives are not worth mentioning.

"However, a great man's life of wisdom is truly valuable, and can last forever. Also, it can be an example for our offspring to follow."

Speaking About One's Mindset

A guest asked: "After reading the first volume of *Still Thoughts,* I realize that you have a whole set of philosophical principles. Asia Week magazine depicted you as a mountain climber.

"May I ask you to describe any changes in your mindset that occurred when you went mountain climbing over the last ten years?"

The Master answered: "Each of us has his own goal in life.

"Before setting that goal, we should consider it carefully and then make a good choice. After setting the goal,

177

we should march toward it resolutely. I want to give you a good explanation by using an analogy: There are two routes by which one can go from the Pure Abode Compound to the Tzu Chi Hospital, the main road or the country road. I can go to the hospital on either. However, I often go on the small country road. The reason is simple; I enjoy watching the beautiful scenery along it.

"I have experienced all sorts of obstacles in my endeavors over the decades. I have always regarded those troubles as scenery along the road, and I have tried to deal with them with a calm attitude.

"When we go mountain climbing, our eventual goal is to climb to the top of the mountain. We should not let the scenery along our way cause us to stray from our goal."

The guest then asked: "If a person likes to help the poor and appreciate the beautiful scenery along the road at the same time, will these two contradict each other?"

The Master answered: "They won't if you feel at ease. It depends on your mindset."

The guest continued: "Were you inspired by things or

people that you experienced before you converted to Buddhism?"

The Master answered: "I hardly have time to look backward or forward. I only live for today."

The guest asked: "The spiritual careers of the Tzu Chi Association will be carried on forever. How can we keep them operating smoothly?"

The Master replied: "Buddha's philosophy teaches us the concept of Karma; a good cause breeds a good effect. What happens to you now can be attributed to things you did in the past, and what you will achieve in the future is based on the endeavors you make at this very moment. Thus, do not daydream about the future; you should work hard right now. Take the Tzu Chi Hospital and the Cultural Center as two examples. We completed these two big construction projects through enormous determination and hard work."

STILL THOUGHTS

Another visitor asked: "Why do living beings have to suffer so much pain?"

The Master responded: "You suffer a lot of pain if you do not have a clear understanding of life. However, you will be very much at ease if you possess a clear understanding. Buddha says, 'Everyone is born equal, and each of us has some Buddhist nature.' You can become as good as Buddha if you are willing to improve yourself constantly.

"You also need to be as helpful and kind to others as a Bodhisattva in order to become like Buddha. All the unhappiness and difficulty will no longer bother you when you are concerned only about learning Buddha's philosophy and helping living beings to their deliverance."

A member asked: "How should I maintain a healthy mind?"

The Master answered: "Most living beings' minds are like a dirt-covered mirror. You should constantly wipe your mind clean with Buddha's philosophy."

A member commented: "I want to thank you for helping me remove my superstitious beliefs. Now my family is doing fine and my husband's career is going very well."

The Master said: "If we intend to remove the bad habits of others, we should first remove our own. Each of us has a different kind of character, just as we have different faces. We often say that it is easier to relocate a mountain than to change a man's character.

Actually, we do not need to change our character, since it also contains a Buddha's nature. Imagine what we would be if we removed Buddha's nature from our characters. What we should really remove is our bad habits."

A member asked: "Is there a real paradise and hell?"

The Master answered: "You are living in a paradise when you behave kindly toward others, but you are living in hell when you behave maliciously."

A member asked the Master to help him cultivate wisdom.

The Master replied: "A person will never be able to cultivate wisdom if he is heartless and cruel. You should try to eliminate all the unnecessary worries from your mind, for they will overshadow the bright side of your heart. How can you maintain a reasonable and wise mind under that condition?"

A member asked: "How should I get rid of my stubborn attachments to things?"

The Master answered: "There are two ways to eliminate one's egotism. First, you should try to minimize your role to become as small as a human cell. Second, you should try to expand yourself to become as big as the universe. You will then be able to accommodate all sorts of people and things by utilizing either way. It is easy to say so, but it is extremely difficult to put this into practice. As we often say: "we should strengthen our will-power by dealing with all sorts of problems."

A member said, "Master, I am sick all over my body. However, the doctor said I was all right after he checked me out. But you see I'm really too sick to work and..."

The Master interrupted to say: "Oh, you are truly sick, and it is too serious to be cured."

"I am?" the startled member said.

The Master replied: "Yes you are. You are indeed sick mentally. No one can cure your mental illness except yourself. But a mental illness will turn into a physical one if you do not take action to stop it. If you wait too long, you will truly be hopeless."

A secular Buddhist devotee spoke about geomancy.

The Master responded: "We Buddhists are concerned only about people's minds, not about geomancy."

STILL THOUGHTS

What are the most beautiful and least beautiful things in the world?

To this often-asked question the Master answered: "A loving heart is the most beautiful thing, while a lustful thought is the least beautiful thing in the world."

A member who happened to be sitting face-to-face with the Master in a meeting felt shy and grabbed a book to look at as a way to shield her face. By coincidence, a Buddha's photo was printed on the book cover. Aware of this, the Master said to her: "I hope you always exhibit a face like Buddha's when blocking out an ordinary person's face."

A guest said: "I am very absent-minded. Whenever I try to do one thing, my concentration strays to another matter. How can I learn to concentrate my mind?"

The Master answered: "You can concentrate your mind by knowing how to use time properly and how to seize the day. Be sure to concentrate your attention on the work you are doing now. Be ready to do a good job when any chance comes, just as a roc (a fabulous, enormous bird) flies high into the sky when a strong wind blows. Working carefully is a habit, not a gesture."

The guest continued: "Since working carefully is merely a habit, why do I need to concentrate my mind? Aren't these two contradictory?"

The Master replied: "When you become used to working carefully, you do not need to pay attention to whether or not you are concentrating. You can walk or eat easily; do you need to concentrate your mind when doing so?"

The guest said: "That sounds very reasonable. However, it is easier to understand this sort of reasoning than to actually put it into practice."

The Master responded: "It is not difficult when you truly understand the reason. It is difficult only when you assume it is difficult."

---

hy is our society in turmoil? Whenever something unexpected happens, people become anxious and fearful.

To this concern the Master said: "This is so because there is a lack of conscience and fair judgment in our society. People tend to act inappropriately when they are filled with biased judgments."

A member asked: "Master, are you confident about Taiwan's future?"

The Master answered: "We must be sincere and confident.

"Everything has some sort of flaw. But if we abandon the challenge, the flaw might get even worse. We should not neglect the big family that is our society for the benefit of our own smaller families."

Speaking About Life

One member asked about the concept of life.

The Master said: "Following is the correct concept of life: You must be responsible for every word you say. Be aware of the goal you are planning at the present time, but do not let worries over the things that might happen tomorrow deter you from pursuing your goal in life. We should plan for the future, yet be attentive to what we are engaged in right now."

Someone said: "Master, your memory is declining because you are too busy and take care of too many things."

The Master replied: "A man's physical body and memory will become poorer and poorer as he gets older, even if he has been lazy all his life and accomplished nothing. Age, not hard work, slow the functions of our bodies. That is why we should seize the day."

What is a fulfilling life?

To this often-asked question the Master said: "To have a fulfilling life, we should respect our superiors and have a loving attitude toward our subordinates. I believe other people will respect us if we treat them with love and courtesy. It is a fulfilling life, if we respect and love one another."

A member asked: "How can I help myself and other people as well?"

The Master said: "You can help yourself

by eliminating your faults, and you can help others by influencing them to correct their own faults."

Speaking About Tolerating Insults

A member said: "Master, I want to be your good disciple. However, the more I tolerate a certain person's insults, the more he seeks to benefit from the situation by trying to gain a yard after taking an inch. My anger is on the verge of exploding. What should I do?"

The Master answered: "Try to regard that man as Buddha who arranges various types of distress just to test you. How could you be angry with Buddha, since you want to imitate his behavior?"

STILL THOUGHTS

A member asked: "How can a person be flexible yet thorough in manner?"

The Master answered: "When you want to dissuade others from doing something bad, you should adopt a flexible and complete manner.

"By doing so, you avoid the risk of being hated by them. We should accommodate the bad people, while guarding against their misconduct."

S omeone asked the Master to talk about the importance of tolerance and patience.

The Master said: "Of the six virtues, tolerance is most important. The friction between people is caused by a lack of tolerance and patience. A man can never cultivate the other five virtues--unselfish giving, abiding by the Buddhist disciplines, self-improvement, meditation, and wisdom--without having cultivated tolerance. You need to be tolerant and patient in order to do things that benefit all living creatures. Each living creature has a different nature. If we want to help living creatures remove their bad habits, we need to wait patiently for the right moment. We can then accomplish our task as easily as skimming oil off the surface of a pool of water. When a person is tolerant and patient, he is able to deal with people smoothly and reasonably. Thus, he can promote the six virtues without expending too much effort."

A member asked: "What kind of people do you feel less compelled to forgive when they offend you?"

The Master said: "I can forgive anyone who is rude to me except those who lie. To err is human, but when a man is dishonest, he is unpardonable."

Speaking About Mercy

n 80-year-old gentleman told the Master: "My grandson said I look younger than before. Is this possible?"

The Master replied: "It is because your heart is filled with love. A loving heart is a beautiful heart that not only breeds happiness among the people around you, but also purifies your body and mind as well as their bodies and minds."

Some members of the Tzu Chi Association often pray to Buddha and his disciples for blessings and good fortune for all the people of the world.

The Master commented: "Besides praying to them, you should also perform good deeds, abide by human ethics, respect the old and love the small children in order to fulfill your wishes. If people continue to commit crimes, how then can they obtain good fortune?"

A perplexed member asked: "Master, why do we feel so happy whenever we meet you? And Master, why does my own son always talk back to me so rudely?"

The Master answered: "These situations are because the Karma (fated opportunity to meet) between you and me will be continued for many lives, whereas the Karma between you and your son is limited for this life only."

The member continued: "If the Karma between you and me will be continued for many lives, then why am I

195

only a secular disciple of yours?"

The Master replied: "It is because you have too many worldly desires, which cause you to become lost."

A secular Buddhist disciple asked: "What is the difference between mercy and universal love?"

The Master answered: "Mercy is much more profound. It requires us to love those with whom we do not have a special relationship, and to have the compassion to share in the unhappiness of others. Mercy is concerned with all living creatures, while universal love covers only human beings."

Today's young people like to drive fast.

To this the Master commented: "Driving fast does not mean you are a good driver, whereas driving slowly shows that you are a polite gentleman. Besides, you should drive slowly in order to protect the Bodhisattva in your heart."

Many people wonder how they can eliminate worries and troubles.

To them the Master commented: "You need to better understand Buddhist philosophy, reduce worldly desires, and extend your love to all living beings in order to eliminate worry."

A student asked: "Is it impolite to read the books written by the Master while lying in bed?"

The Master answered, "Politeness is demonstrated by more than your actions. True politeness is when you take my words seriously and put them into practice in your daily conduct."

A member asked: "How do you define real love?"

The Master answered: "Wisdom is the prerequisite for a pure love that is without self-consideration and desire. I define real love as when we offer our pure love even to people with whom we do not have a special relationship, and when we have the compassion to

STILL THOUGHTS

share in the unhappiness of others."

Speaking About Daily Affairs

A member asked: "Why do members of the Tzu Chi Association like to talk about and praise their own association? Are they bragging?"

The Master answered: "In Buddhism, each Buddha has his own realm. Take the Amitabha (the Buddha of Infinite Light) for instance:

"He is determined to help deliver all living beings. If we chant his holy name often, we will be ushered into his realm at the moment we die. The same can be applied to the Buddha of Medicine. The Tzu Chi world is indeed beautiful, and praiseworthy. We do not tarnish its good reputa-

199

tion simply by praising its accomplishments."

(Editor's note: Everyone in the Tzu Chi world is kind in thought, behavior and speech. All the members have contributed much toward preserving the land of beauty, goodness and truth for our children. Isn't it wonderful!)

 A member said: "I was wondering if I should take my children to visit impoverished families."

The Master answered: "That's fine. Take them as if it was a picnic. As such, you will be letting them know what we Tzu Chi people are doing. Besides, it will be a good opportunity to teach them about gratitude; many children realize how lucky and wealthy they are after visiting poor families. They will better appreciate what they have. But there is one very important thing of which you must remind your children: be gentle to the poor. Complaining about the filthy living conditions of the poor is forbidden. Adults cannot allow their children to become spoiled."

A group of Tzu Chi members performed an aboriginal dance at a celebration. Everyone was dancing and joyful.

A member asked: "Master, you said we danced so well it was as if we were actually aborigines. Did you also mean to imply we were unsophisticated?"

The Master answered: "The word 'unsophisticated' also implies purity and innocence. If someone criticizes you as being keen and sharp, he might really be meaning to say that you are very cunning. You should ponder the possibilities."

A visitor stated: "The Tzu Chi people seem to be rich?"

The Master responded: "They are not only well off financially, but also rich in love, wisdom and compassion!"

STILL THOUGHTS

A member said: "Master, I want to take part in Tzu Chi's charitable activities more frequently. However, I was worried that I might become too famous by doing so, and the prominent people are more open to attack."

The Master answered: "It is appropriate for you to become famous while developing the function of your life to help others. You will not be open to attack if you constantly watch your manner."

One member began to say: "Master, our Tzu Chi Association has become very famous. It is known to many people ..."

But the Master interrupted with: "Yes! And we should be careful to maintain its good reputation."

(Editor's note: It is difficult to start any kind of operation, and harder still to maintain its functioning. The Spiritual Careers of the Tzu Chi Association still need everyone's support.)

A member asked: "The scale of the spiritual careers of the Tzu Chi Association is very large now. What should we do when you are gone?"

The Master grew silent and speechless, before responding in a sentimental tone: "Why do people always worry about death? Why don't they simply seize the day and do what they must."

(Editor's note: Life is filled with changes. Many people were worried about the Master's health 20 years ago. However, the Master has provided unflagging devotion to the spiritual careers of the Tzu Chi Association over the past two decades, helping the poor and enlightening her disciples. Many members of Tzu Chi have come and gone during this period of time, with the Master remaining resolute in pursuing her goals. Who knows, you and I may not be here after another 20 years and the Master may be working still, devoting her energy and enthusiasm to promoting Tzu Chi's charitable activities.

Is it not true that Buddha's spirit has been carried on from generation to generation over the last 2,000 years?)

STILL THOUGHTS

O ne member noted: "We donated a lot of money to build the Tzu Chi Hospital in Hualien. However, some of us cannot use the facility very easily because it is located too far away. Do you think that is unfortunate for us?"

The Master answered: "Out of the eight ways to create good fortune, helping patients care for their illnesses is the most important one. The reason we set up the hospital in eastern Taiwan was because that part of the island lacked medical facilities. A Buddhist should strive to be a big-hearted person. Realize that any hospital is constructed to serve the needs of the sick people. Isn't it wonderful that you don't need it?"

A member said to the Master: "Thank you so much for re-educating my wife. She has become more gentle, diligent and thoughtful since she became a member of the Tzu Chi Association."

The Master said: "It was not I who re-educated your

wife and other members. After joining the association, many people have experienced the unhappy side of life, such as witnessing illness or death. They now realize that life is filled with changes. These experiences constantly remind them of how short life is, and how important it is to correct their wrong behavior. We can often learn from interacting with a group of people. I really appreciate the support of our members' spouses; they have been a big help to me."

A guest asked: "You have instituted a rule that all donations must be used on Tzu Chi's charitable activities, while you and others who live in the pure abode compound rely only on what you produce.

"Was this a decision you made when you first became a nun? If so, why?"

The Master answered: "I have always abided by the 'earn one's own living' rule, even before I became a nun. I still live by that rule. To stand on my own feet is one of two principles I pursue. The other is unselfish giving. Our association's accomplishments can be attributed to the accumulation of each member's donations and unselfish giving. After establishing the Tzu Chi Association, I was careful to separate donated funds from operating funds. What our association has achieved today is based on the members' sincerity and honesty. We should never allow any careless mistake or character flaw tarnish the association's good reputation."

A member asked: "What should we do to convince others to convert to Buddhism?"

The Master answered: "Buddha introduced his religion to the world for the sake of saving living beings. Buddha has to serve the living beings first before he can let them understand Buddhism. That is why we Tzu Chi members first become devoted to our four spiritual careers in order to do good things for the living beings. We can then introduce them to Buddhism."

A member questioned: "The Master's resolution is great, but what should we disciples do to help realize it?"

The Master answered: "A centipede has a hundred legs that are well coordinated with one another. We must be of one mind and concert our efforts. Then, we will certainly realize our goals."

O ne member asked: "What should we do when a poor patient is hospitalized for a long time without paying the bill?"

The Master answered: "I keep telling the doctors at the hospital that it is their job to look after the poor patients, and my job to take care of the bills. Poor patients can go to the Social Welfare Department at the hospital. They can enjoy either a discount or completely free diagnosis and treatment if meeting our criteria. Also, we should encourage patients who only have domestic problems to stand on their own two feet. They can pay for bills in installments after finding work."

A member confided: "Master, I am so moved by the things accomplished by Tzu Chi. I wish I could help more, but my physical condition is weak. I have lots of problems."

The Master replied: "The fact that our physical conditions become poor is why we must realize we do not have time to waste. Our body is a vehicle for carrying out our religious faith. We can achieve meritorious deeds if we sincerely want to."

A member asked: "What if each of us made a wish to become a Tzu Chi medical doctor in the next life? Would we have enough patients to look after?"

The Master answered: "People sometimes are unhealthy mentally, instead of physically. We need good doctors who can be as benevolent as a Bodhisattva to cure people's psychological illnesses."

A visitor asked: "What is the most profound significance of the four spiritual careers of the Tzu Chi Association?"

The Master responded: "The most profound significance of the four spiritual careers of charity, medicine, education and culture is that we put our ideals into action. The development of Tzu Chi's spiritual careers must be based on proper action-taking. It would be useless if we did not put our magnificent ideals into action. Yet, it would be impossible for us to put our ideals into action without doing so via the proper way."

A nother visitor questioned: "Buddha says, 'Less desire, more contentment.' Tzu Chi's spiritual careers are getting bigger and bigger. Is it against Buddha's instruction to have many desires?"

The Master answered: "There are two different types of desires.

"The first category comprises those involving the imitation of the saints' behavior. The second kind are those for evil pleasures, such as the desire for wealth, wanton sex, fame, lavish food and idle sleeping."

A member said: "Master, I tried to introduce Tzu Chi to a rich man in the hope that he would join us to do good things. He said he wasn't interested and turned me down."

The Master answered: "The work of Tzu Chi needs to be done by people with a volunteer spirit. We should introduce our work to everyone, no matter rich or poor. We should let them know that our association is a good place for making meritorious contributions. We can congratulate those who are willing to join us, but we should not express disappointment toward those who are unwilling."

Speaking About Learning

A member asked: "How can we learn from Buddha's wisdom in order to avoid growing attached to things?"

The Master answered: "You should not become attached to things, since you know this is wrong. People are too smart to be fooled or taken advantage of. Ironically, they fail to perceive the simplicity of human affairs."

A member said: "I have been busy soliciting donations everywhere. Therefore, I have not had that much time to read sutras."

211

STILL THOUGHTS

The Master said: "Everything that happens in our lives is a form of the living sutras, all of which helps us cultivate our wisdom. We can never apprehend Buddha's philosophy by reading sutras only. We need to cultivate a state of quietness and peacefulness by dealing with different problems or people."

A member asked: "What is the proper way of learning?"

The Master answered: "You need to read carefully, listen carefully, think carefully, and skillfully apply what you have learned when you deal with problems or people."

Speaking About Time

A member asked: "Master, why are you always reminding us to make good use of every second?"

The Master answered: "Life is filled with changes, and our lives depend on the air we breathe. Life would cease if we could not breathe. That is why we need to make good use of each second."

The member continued: "Master, do you have any plans for the future?"

The Master replied: "I have some plans, but it is important for me to seize the day. I must make good use of

213

STILL THOUGHTS

my 86,400 seconds each day."

Speaking About Management

A guest said: "It is a traditional Chinese concept to emphasize ethics, and rule by benevolence and propriety. But we can no longer rely solely on the spirit of tradition when coping with our social turmoils. To manage and govern our society, we need a whole set of regulations and laws that meet the requirements of social justice. I am writing a book about countries ruled by law. Could you please give me some advice?"

The Master answered: "We cannot live without law. Civic regulations are one kind of law, while moral regulations are another.

STILL THOUGHTS

"Unlike the former, which are a temporary remedy for social problems, the latter are fundamental. Formal regulations set penalties for wrong behavior, whereas moral regulations help us build up a nature of self-discipline. In order to write a good book about countries ruled by law, you must specify your angle of elaboration."

A member asked: "Master, how do you control your subordinates?"

The Master answered: "It is very hard to control other people. People, in fact, do not like to be controlled by someone else. The best method of personnel management is to let people develop a good mindset of self-discipline."

Speaking About Doing Work

A member asked: "Have you come to a conclusion regarding what you have accomplished over the last 25 years?"

The Master answered: "My conclusion is that I did just what I should have done. My mind would be in a state of confusion if I kept looking back on what I did, and would be in a state of delusion if I kept dreaming about the future. On the other hand, I certainly must continue to seize the day, marching toward my goals in accordance with my blueprint."

secular disciple asked: "I have often performed many good things for others. Even so, why is it that I cannot achieve greatness in my business or my morality-cultivation?"

The Master answered: "You need to make a proper choice in doing good things. Buddha's sutras talk about the ten evil ways, such as the devil of good deeds and the devil of confidence. You would be easily fooled by the devil of good deeds if you did not make a wise choice in the deeds you choose to do. Don't keep telling yourself that your business will be great simply because you have done so much for the poor. If you do, you will bring worry to yourself each time you perform good things for others. That is why we depict people such as you as being fooled by the devil of good deeds. You cannot improve your morality by being so."

guest said: "Some people call you Taiwan's 'Mother Teresa' or its 'Albert Schweitzer,' or a great Bodhisattva that came into the world to fulfill her will for saving people. What do you think?"

The Master said: "I just do what I should do."

One member is regarded as having become smug and complacent after receiving high praise from others in the Tzu Chi Association for his outstanding contribution to the group.

Of him, the Master said: "He is not praiseworthy. Who is more praiseworthy -- the man who is capable of carrying a burden that weighs 10 kilos yet carries only eight, or the man who is only capable of carrying one kilo, but strains as best he can to bear a burden that weighs one and a half kilos?"

(Editor's note: There are some senior members in the Tzu Chi Association who cannot read very many words. Even so, they abide by the Master's instructions to help others quietly. For this, they are truly praiseworthy.)

STILL THOUGHTS

A guest asked: "It is difficult to ask others to join in one's work. However, we often need the help of others in order to complete our tasks. How can we motivate others to join us to work together joyfully?"

The Master responded: "If you want to gain something, you must first give unselfishly to others. You will never gain what you want if you are too demanding. The reason life may seem tough is because you may be demanding something you do not deserve to have."

A member asked: "Can we refuse to do a job when we feel it is beyond our capabilities?"

The Master answered: "A real gentleman will try everything he can to improve himself, despite any hardship or difficulty. Nothing is impossible if we work diligently. There is a Chinese saying that goes, 'A gentleman will never abandon a chance to do something good for others.' How, then, can you refuse to do a job that will benefit others?"

A member commented: "It is very hard to make oneself popular among people. It is so easy to offend them."

The master responded: "The reason you cannot get along with others smoothly is because you sometimes talk too much when you should keep silent, and sometimes keep your mouth closed tight when you should be stating your opinion."

(Editor's note: A man often gets himself into trouble when he speaks inappropriately.)

One member asked: "I have trouble controlling my bad temper. What should I do?

The master replied: "A bad temper will not only bother yourself, but also make you a nuisance to others. A good temper will not only bring you happiness, but make you more popular. A man's personality and sense of morality depend on whether he has a good or bad temper. A man's bad temper will ruin his good personality, even though he may be an honorable person."

Speaking About Vexations

 member stated: "I am working in a beauty parlor. The busier I am, the more meaningless I feel life is."

The Master answered: "You probably lack quality in your life. That is why you feel life is meaningless. You can fill your life with Buddha's philosophy. You can listen to sutras recorded on tapes while serving your customers. In doing so, you will be not only cleaning hair, but also purifying hearts. You can also set a goal for your life."

A member asked: "I have been reading sutras daily and I also understand the importance of morality-cultivation. But why do I still have plenty of worries?"

The Master responded: "I can help those who do not understand Buddha's philosophy. But since you know Buddha's philosophy and sutras and still cannot find peace and relaxation, there is nothing I can do for you."

The member continued: "I am never able to let worries just slide off my shoulder.

The Master replied: "It is beyond Buddha's ability to help you if you keep thinking this way. You should correct your mindset since you already know it is wrong."

A hospital nurse is often irritated about having to work in the operating room with a famous but bad-tempered doctor.

To her the Master said: "Try to deal with the doctor with a sense of humor. Let him vent his resentment and then comfort him with gentle words. I believe his mind will gradually become peaceful."

A n entrepreneur complained: "My career is pretty successful. I own everything I want. But why do I still feel life is meaningless?"

The Master said: "Ordinary people focus too much attention on themselves. They tend to become greedy and too ambitious. When they have earned 10 million dollars, they want to earn 30 million. They are never content with what they have. Buddha says, 'Stability is the greatest interest, and contentment is the greatest fortune.' You will be happier if you share the fruits of what you have harvested with others. Do not forget that you are a member of society. You cannot accomplish anything great without the support of other people. Besides, you cannot take any material things along with you at the moment you go to meet Buddha."

Speaking About Desires

 member asked: "Master, were you born with your perseverance, courage and confidence? Or, were you forced to become so?"

The Master answered: "A person's strength will be boundless when he is not after something he does not deserve to have. Preoccupation with trivia saps one's spirit, perseverance and courage."

 guest confided: "I learned a lot about your achievements even before I came to see you in Hualien. I am very happy to see you today. I have been exposed to various religions since I was 20 years old, but I never felt like I belonged to any particular one.

"Fortunately, I have read your books and am inspired by your wise words. Also, I am deeply impressed by your sense of accommodation and your spirit of perseverance. You have successfully freed yourself from both the bondage of secular rules and the restrictions of religion. Consequently, more people have come to participate in your charitable activities. The gap between people, to a great extent, has been eliminated. This, to me, is the most important of the great things you have achieved."

The Master responded: "I only let nature take its course. I do not accommodate people with something deliberate in mind."

The guest continued: "This is what touched my heart the most.

"Your manner is so natural and humble when you talk about the things you have been doing."

The Master said: "It is natural for fish to live in water and humans to breathe the air. To accommodate others is also part of the natural elements. Being members of society, we should care about and accept one another naturally. People nowadays behave in unnatural ways. That is why they regard something natural as abnormal."

Speaking About Social Customs

A n attorney said to the Master: "Our social customs are no longer good. It is painful to see a group of relatives sue one another in order to fight for money."

The Master said: "From a religious person's perspective, I feel the fewer trials the better. The fewer trials we engage in, the more time we will have to achieve meritorious deeds. It is painful to go through a legal process, whether you win or lose."

A secular Buddhist disciple asked for the Master's opinion about stock market investing.

The Master answered: "It's a good thing when you enhance a society's interflow of capital and property by buying and selling stocks. But when you speculate on the stock exchange in an opportunistic way, you not only make others suffer from the ups and downs of prices, but also make yourself lazy and greedy. When judging from the Buddhist concept of cause and effect, I can call people who speculate on the stock market 'real trouble-makers,' even though they might not intentionally mean to 'bring ruin to other people or their own families.'"

A visitor asked: "Our society is filled with many problems. What is the major cause?"

The Master answered: "Each individual of our society should be held accountable. If we want to make our nation strong, each of us must assume responsibility. The garbage disposal problem, for example, exists because each family creates too much waste, not because there is no place to put the accumulating rubbish."

What are the Tzu Chi members' responsibilities?
The Master elaborated: "There are two things that need to be done by Tzu Chi commissioners and members: help the poor, and educate the rich. All of the rich are not necessarily loving people. Buddha says that each of us has a loving heart. People, however, have become habitually selfish, and they are concerned only about their own families. They tend to do whatever they can to earn a lot of money, but it is hard to say whether they will be willing to share their gains with others. Some people lose what they achieve and become the burden of other people's support and contributions. Individuals and society are closely linked. A man will never share the results of his successes with others when he is selfish. Imagine what our society would be like if everyone was selfish. It is the Tzu Chi commissioners' duty to educate the rich and to cultivate within them a loving heart. Fine grains of sand as they accumulate make a pagoda.

"It would swell into such a great power if we could accumulate rich people's contributions."

How can we resolve the confrontations between labor and management?

On this issue, the Master said: "In the past, people worked to live. They were worried about being fired by their boss. The tables are turning now; the bosses are worried about losing their careers.

In order to be a good manager, you should get rid of the 'I'm the president, you're the employee' boss mentality."

A member asked: "How can I distinguish between complexity and simplicity?"

The Master answered: "Simplicity can be very complex, and complexity can be very simple. Eating is a simple task, but you can choke to death if you eat carelessly."

Section Two: About Religion
Speaking About Cause and Effect

A member asked, "I have never seen 'cause.' What is it?"

The Master answered: "'Cause' is like a seed of longan. If I told you the seed was a longan tree, you would not believe me because it would be viewed merely as a seed from any perspective.

"This is what we mean when we say 'a cause without Karma.' But the seed will grow, bloom and eventually bear fruit after we put it in the ground. A kind heart of unselfish giving is like a seed. You should seize the right opportunity to plant the seed, so that it can grow into a big tree. And you should wait patiently for the results.

"Do not think you are going to reap the fruit the very next day after you plant the seed. You might ruin the seed completely if you dig it up to see whether it is still alive."

A member asked: "Why do some people live a comfortable life even though they have never done anything good?"

The Master answered: "We need to discuss the Karma of one's previous three lives in order to respond to your question. We often meet two groups of people: those who are kind and nice toward others, and those who are bossy and cruel toward others. However, people of the former group sometimes have rougher lives than the latter. Why?

"It is because of the Karma decided in their previous lives. Although Karma is something we cannot change, we can be completely at ease if we face Karma calmly and take Buddha's philosophy as our spiritual support."

STILL THOUGHTS

A member questioned: "I have always behaved properly in my life. Even so, why do many things not always turn out the way I wish?"

The Master responded: "You are doing pretty well now. However, the good effect has not shown up yet. All the unpleasant matters you are facing now can be attributed to the unfavorable cause made in the past. Cause is a seed."

A n entrepreneur asked: "I have never done any-thing bad as an adult. But I have encountered a series of unlucky incidents recently. I am quite puzzled and nervous. I cannot help but seek the help of a fortune-teller."

The Master answered: "It is our duty to act properly. Most people in the world do not do bad things throughout their lives. However, they seldom do anything good, either. It is nothing special if you do not do bad things to others. But it is important to do things that benefit others in order to change your Karma and fate. It is useless to have good intentions yet never put them into practice."

Speaking About Eliminating Disaster

A member asked: "Master, when is you birthday?"

The Master answered: "Each new day to me is like a birthday.

"The moment I open my eyes in the morning is a new beginning for me to treat others sincerely."

A member asked: "How can I eliminate misfortune and increase my good fortune?"

The Master answered: "It all depends on you. You must cultivate virtue in order to eliminate disaster. You can avoid confronting others by giving in a little. You can change a potential disaster into an incident of good fortune by showing a gentle, loving attitude."

P eople often ask the Master how they can increase their good fortune.

The Master tells them: "You can increase the abundance of good fortune for yourself by doing things that benefit others."

Speaking About Superstition

A member said: "I wanted to place my mother's ashes in a pagoda.

"At first, I did not know which spot I should put them in, so I asked for Buddha's opinion."

The Master responded with a question: "How did you ask him?"

The man replied: "I asked him by throwing chao-pei (wooden divination cups) on the ground. He liked my choice."

The Master said: "You are wrong. It was you, not Buddha, who chose the good spot for your mother's ashes.

Buddha would never convey a message to you via those two pieces of wood. In fact, it was you who conveyed the message to yourself by using the wooden cups."

A nother member asked: "Why do so many Buddhists like to have their fortune predicted by throwing the wooden divination cups before gods in a temple?"

The Master answered: "Many people blindly believe in the fortune-telling function of those two pieces of wood. In fact, it is better for you to not have any religious faith at all, than to blindly believe in a religion. To believe blindly can be destructive.

"Often, people become rational and faithful once they perceive the truth of religion. However, people who blindly believe in a religion tend to always make far-fetched decisions. The consequences are often destructive."

STILL THOUGHTS

A member asked: "Can we eliminate bad Karma by chanting sutras?"

The Master replied: "There would be no cause and effect if we eliminated bad Karma by chanting sutras. Being human, we will all die someday; you must get off the bus at the station stop that corresponds with the mileage you paid for when you bought your ticket. You should do things beneficial to others prior to any arrival of bad Karma."

A man said: I have suffered from an undetermined illness since I had a car accident. I'm very confused and uneasy because I can't figure out what's going on. I often pray to the gods in any temple I come across."

The Master answered: "You should not believe in any religion you hear about. Make a well-thought-out decision. Choose an orthodox religion. Any religion should perform an educational function in its spiritual sublimation. Churches and temples should be places for learning about human affairs. You must relax first, and then you will be able to calm down. The so-called demons will leave you alone when you are in a quiet state of peacefulness. They exist nowhere but in your heart. We Buddhists believe in the concept of the unavoidable Karma. Whether you like it or not, the fated things in our lives are destined to happen no matter what. Try to accept any unfortunate episodes along the way with a joyful attitude, because they will soon pass."

A member asked: "When we face a problem, should we use divination or beseech the gods for help?"

The Master answered: "Face the reality bravely and resolutely. We should remain joyful, even when under the challenge of distress. You can get yourself into big trouble by blindly seeking help from gods or divination practitioners, because they might confuse you or mislead you into making a wrong decision."

Speaking About Faith

Someone asked: "I have heard the expression, 'Be concerned as if you were not.' What does it mean?"

The Master answered: "We should always be concerned about Buddha, not ourselves. And, we should do this in a natural manner."

A member said: "Someone suggested that I prostrate myself before the Sutra of Earth-treasury."

The Master said: "It would be better if you made a resolution that was as noble as the one made by the Bodhisattva of Earth-treasury, than if you prostrated yourself before the sutra written by him. It is the Buddha in your heart that you should worship, not some printed materials. All the sutras are like roads that lead you to the realm of the saints. Don't hesitate to walk on these roads, even though you cherish them very much."

nother member asked: "Someone told me I should chant the Goddess of Mercy's name before 12 a.m., and Amitabha's name after 12 a.m. Is this appropriate?"

The Master answered: "It makes no difference, as long as you concentrate your mind on chanting their names. You will enhance your merciful feeling toward others by chanting the Goddess of Mercy's name. You will increase your capacity for tolerance, trust and sense of accommodation by chanting Amitabha's name. By achieving a strong sense of accommodation, you will be able to acquire a great deal of good fortune. You will have a bright future if you are merciful toward others."

243

STILL THOUGHTS

A member questioned: "Will our problems be resolved if we beg Bodhisattvas for help?"

The Master responded: "All living creatures are under the great influence of Karma, and each human being has some kind of worry in his deepest heart. If you pray devoutly to Bodhisattvas for help, they will mercifully inspire or teach you the right method to eliminate your worries. Buddhism has a profound function of education. You will become stronger and more resolute once you accept it sincerely. However you should not always turn to Buddha for help when you are in trouble. The best solution for overcoming troubles is to be confident and resolute within yourself. Those are strengths you can always count on."

A member asked: "I believe in Buddha, and I often go to a temple to worship him and study his sutras. Should I do so everyday?"

The Master answered: "It is not necessary. The fundamental way to show that you have faith in Buddhism is to demonstrate your determination to imitate Buddha's behavior. You would not be a good Buddhist if you worshiped Buddha yet did not imitate his behavior."

A member complained: "My husband disapproves of my worship of Buddha."

The Master responded: "The worshipping of Buddha and chanting of sutras are merely methods to help us improve our knowledge. Your family would certainly disapprove of your belief, if you spent all your time chanting sutras in a temple without improving your moral culture, stubbornness and superstition. Religion is something that can enlighten us so that we can eliminate our egoism. After hearing your husband's complaints, you should re-examine your behavior from his point of view. This is the essence of true love and the duty of a Buddhist."

STILL THOUGHTS

Someone asked: "What is the difference between the concepts of Sakyamuni and Amitabha?"

The Master answered: "Sakyamuni is the most respected master in Buddhism. We practice the Buddhist conducts in accordance with his teachings. Amitabha teaches us to forget all worldly concerns and try to perceive the Western World of Perfect Happiness (Paradise). If we maintain clean minds, the whole territory of our nation will also be clean. The whole world would be a paradise, if all of our minds became pure."

A member asked: "I don't think I have enough insight to perceive the wisdom Buddha recorded in his sutras. What should I do?"

The Master answered: "You should chant Buddha's sutras until your heart has become as benevolent as Buddha's. You will then become as wise as Buddha. Buddha's heart is one filled with great mercy and compassion."

Speaking About Imitating Buddha's Behavior

A visitor commented: "Someone has encouraged me to leave home and become a monk. However, I often have random thoughts and hear unreal sounds. I tried to get rid of them by chanting Buddhist words of exorcism, but the result was even worse."

The Master replied: "It is not necessary for you to become a monk if you want to imitate Buddha's behavior. It will not do you any good to become a monk when you still have a lot of random thoughts.

"Some people try very hard to imitate Buddha's behavior, treating their parents nicely, promoting Buddha's philosophy, and so forth.

"These people are not monks or nuns, but they successfully achieve their goal of imitating Buddha's good behavior. They are what we call 'indoor' Bodhisattvas. Buddhism is a lively yet relaxing religion, but we must be certain to believe in orthodox Buddhism. You should refrain from meditating and chanting words of exorcism unless you have found a good instructor. And, you should turn a deaf ear to the unreal sounds; they will eventually fade. The sounds you hear are, in fact, your own mental attachments. That is why you are able to hear them."

A member asked: "How can we perceive Buddha's philosophy?"

The Master answered: "You should learn from Buddha's teachings as much as possible, dwell upon them, live by them and, above all, implement them with practical actions. You will perceive Buddha's philosophy after doing all this. You will then be free from worry and much wiser."

A member asked: "Will our belief in Buddhism damage our family life?"

The Master answered: "It will never damage the happiness of your families; it will never harm the love and romance between husband and wife. A person can better cultivate virtue, manage the family, and help bring peace to the whole world by believing in Buddha and abiding by moral discipline. Those who are able to abide by moral discipline are people with clear minds. They are usually passionate and merciful toward others. How can people like this damage the happiness of their families?"

A student asked: "Is the story about the living Buddha in Chinshan true?"

The Master answered: "What's really worth noting about the living Buddha is his strong capacity of tolerance. He always turns a deaf ear to slander from others, and he remains calm when he is in trouble. These examples, and not the details of his miraculous activities, are what we should learn from him."

A visitor asked: "The Master's spiritual careers have been implemented within a large scale enterprise that is highly admired by thousands of people. This would seem to be a sort of reform and breakthrough in Buddhism."

The Master responded: "Many people say that I am reforming Buddhism, but actually I am reviving its old tradition. When Buddha was alive, he did not have any profound sutras to teach his disciples. He merely utilized the small things happening around him as examples for teaching people how to live happily, treat others nicely, and devote their love to all of society. For certain, he would point out the impoverished living conditions, anguish and social illnesses of the people of India when trying to inspire them.

"I am acting in the same way as did Buddha some 2, 500 years ago. If people think I am reforming Buddhism, I would rather they see my actions as reviving the customs of

Buddha's era."

A visitor said: "Master, you seldom use abstruse words when preaching Buddha's philosophy. Yet, your words are very appealing and convincing."

The Master commented: "The importance of Buddha's philosophy is not its profundity; it simply teaches us how to live a significant and meaningful life. It is closely connected to our lives. This is truly Buddha's religious concept."

A news reporter asked: "What contribution has religion made to social development?"

The Master answered: "Our society needs religion, because only religion can awaken one's conscience. People's desires are like the dirt that can easily cover the good side of human nature. Only religion can wash away the dirt, awaken our conscience, and guide us to develop our innate knowledge and ability."

STILL THOUGHTS

A member asked: "How can we achieve a deep understanding of religion?"

The Master said: "It is a goal that you cannot achieve within one or two days. Buddhism is not a religion that teaches merely about Buddha-worship or Buddhist festivals. In truth, it teaches you how to perceive life's goal and how to act sincerely toward others."

A member asked: "Why don't Buddhists talk about geomancy?"

The Master answered: "Geomancy does exist, even though we Buddhists do not talk about it. In Buddhism, we believe in the concept of Karma, and there are two kinds of Karma -- good and bad.

"A person with a good Karma will find that wherever he goes, he will always be in a nice place. However, when a man has a bad Karma, he will not enjoy living in any particular place, even if that place is highly praised by a geomancer. Righteousness is a virtue that we strive for throughout our lives. Righteousness will afford us a strong

Speaking About Imitating Buddha's Behavior

will-power, as well as bring us luck."

Speaking About Unselfish Giving

A member asked: "Why do rich people seldom participate in charitable activities?"

The Master answered: "The rich people usually lack a strong desire to give what they have unselfishly to others. It is also difficult for them to limit their worldly desires, or to offer their love and compassion to other living creatures. This is because they fail to perceive the truth of life. For this reason, we feel they can hardly cultivate virtue or participate in charitable activities."

A member said: "I would donate a large part of my profit to the Tzu Chi Foundation if I successfully speculated on the stock market."

The Master replied: "We do not have a penny when we come into this world, and we will not take a penny with us when we leave. You would do better to earn your money in a stable way, and donate according to your financial situation. Do not let your emotions fluctuate in accordance with the ups and downs of the shares prices index. If I advised you not to invest in the stock exchange, you would surely thank me when the index falls. But, you would surely complain to me when it goes up. How can you develop your wisdom, when your mood fluctuates according to stock market changes? As well, how then would you be able to muster enough energy to work on other matters? You will have a much cleaner mind when you decide not to earn money in this way."

STILL THOUGHTS

S omeone said: "It's very difficult to earn money, so I never share what I have earned with others."

The Master said: "You should share what you have earned with other people in our society. We should plow the seeds of kindness, so that we can reap rewards and blessings in the future. Judge for yourself: Which is more wise, to help others while you can or to create a bad Karma for yourself by selfishly depositing every penny into a bank? It is a big mistake when you assume the smartest thing to do is that which benefits only yourself."

Speaking About the Practice of Buddhist Rules

A member asked: "We often use one thousand hands and one thousand eyes to describe the capabilities of Buddhas. What is the significance of this?"

The Master answered: "The thousand hands and eyes is a metaphor for perfection. You can see the details of everything with one thousand eyes, and do everything with one thousand hands."

STILL THOUGHTS

H ow can we be reborn to the Western World of Perfect Happiness?

To this often-asked question, the Master usually responds: "You need to make a strong resolution for helping, and cultivate kindness and good fortune in order to reach that goal. You also need to put your good ideas into practice by taking action. The distance between the Western Pure Land and the world we live in is too far to be measured. We cannot reach our destination without practicing good deeds."

C an one get closer to Buddha's philosophy by becoming a monk or nun?

To this, the Master often answers: "This is a matter of fortitude and courage, and you need to cultivate a healthy mind first. After becoming a monk or nun, you should not engage immediately in the glorious task of 'promoting Buddha's philosophy, and helping the living creatures.' You should be happy and satisfied just to know that you can learn how to set yourself free from worry, and that you can get along well with other monks and nuns in your group."

A member stated: "It is such a tough job to help the poor. There are so many we can never help them all. It saddens me when I think of this."

The Master responded: "It is natural for a kind man like you to sympathize with those in trouble and offer them help. Even Buddha could not save and deliver all living creatures. We should therefore try our best to help them whenever possible."

The member continued: "A lot of people have ended up in poverty and misfortune after doing evil things. Can we prevent these people from doing bad things by educating them to Buddha's philosophy?"

The Master said: "Buddhism has been systematically spread among people. Many Buddhist masters have been promoting Buddha's philosophy to help correct people's mistakes. Those who have a Buddhist inclination will naturally become exposed to Buddha's philosophy and thereby have the opportunity to adopt it."

A member asked: "I am considering teaching primary school students how to behave properly, in the hope that they will not commit any crimes when they grow up. Please tell me how I can best fulfill this task?"

The Master answered: "You must be certain to cherish your happy family and carefully educate your own children. On the other hand, it is appropriate for you to take the time to act as a volunteer safety guard at your children's school or at the nursery school in your community. Try to make friends with children; you will then be able to show your love and wisdom to them."

What about the unrecognized good deeds?

To this question, the Master often responds: "You should not expect other people to be aware of all the good deeds you perform. Just be concerned about being helpful.

How can we distinguish the difference between insincere assistance and "giving helpful consideration" as set down in Buddha's philosophy?"

To this, the Master often says: "It is better for us to just do our work earnestly, because these two meanings can be very misleading if you ponder them from the wrong angle."

A member said: "It is the duty of us disciples to serve Buddha, his philosophy, and the monks and nuns. But you refuse to be served by us. Do you think you could be preventing us from obtaining a reward we would deserve for serving you?"

The Master replied: "There are three ways to serve your master: to serve with money, to serve with respect and to serve by implementation. How would it be possible for a Buddhist nun like me to fulfill the four spiritual careers of the Tzu Chi Foundation without your financial support? It is much more significant for you to financially support my eternal life of wisdom, than to help my mortal body.

"Besides, all the commissioners of Tzu Chi have regarded my spiritual careers as their own, following me to fulfill the spiritual careers resolutely. This is serving with respect. Furthermore, you can combine your efforts to help the poor and educate the rich, trying as best you can to carry out Bodhisattva's benevolent wishes through practical actions. This is serving by implementation. If you can perform all the three ways of serving, I would indeed be a master fully served by her disciples."

 member asked: "If a person wants to become a monk or nun, what kind of mentality should he or she have?"

The Master answered: "Try to serve human beings with a positive mentality. A full understanding of the spirit of Buddhism is also needed."

Speaking About the Practice of Buddhist Rules

A member asked: "Why do we need to prostrate ourselves before the Master?"

The Master answered: "All devotees need to pay respect to the three Buddhist treasures of Buddha, his philosophy and the monks and nuns. All the monks and nuns help Buddha promote his philosophy. If you cannot outwardly show your respect for them, how can you sincerely accept what they preach."

A member asked: "Can we offer meat or fish to the Heavenly God as a sacrifice?"

The Master answered: "He will not eat, no matter what kind of food you offer. This is actually an old custom of the agrarian society. People were thrifty, eating simply except on important folk religion festivals. They could enjoy substantial meals after first offering the delicacies to the gods. Instead, fresh flowers, fruit and, above all, a sincere heart may be your best offerings."

STILL THOUGHTS

A foreign friend asked: "I have seen many temples in Taiwan. The temple at the Pure Abode Compound is one of few that does not have exquisite carvings, beautiful statues of Buddha, or colorful decorations. It is in fact very simple and plain. What is it you intend to preserve or eliminate by this?"

The Master answered: "We want to preserve Buddha's spirit, and eliminate the material comforts of life."

The foreign friend continued: "If Buddha's spirit dwells in our mind and our behavior, why do so many religious groups still practice their formal rituals?"

The Master replied: "The invisible religious spirit is often transmitted through rituals. These rituals are a kind of traditional etiquette; they absolutely need to be maintained."

The foreign friend added: "Is it because we are not strong enough that we need the support of etiquette?"

The Master answered: "This is not so. The reason we human beings are different from other animals is because we have developed various kinds of cultures and etiquette.

Religious rituals are a concrete way to perpetuate our cultural foundation. They cannot be abolished."

A member asked about the meaning of the worship of Buddha.

The Master responded: "The meaning of the worship of Buddha lies in training ourselves to be resolute, patient and calm in our minds. Doing so is also a course by which we can develop our capabilities, both physical and mental."

A member commented: "A husband of one of our members has not yet converted to Buddhism, because he is worried other people might say he has been saved and delivered by his wife."

The Master said: "It is nice to be saved and delivered by someone else. 'To save and deliver' is Buddhist phraseology. It means that you influence others by using personal examples of moral uprightness. You can only achieve this end by first correcting your own mistaken ways."

STILL THOUGHTS

A reporter asked: "Is there a lot of difference between people who believe in Buddha and those who do not believe?"

The Master answered: "There is not much difference between the two, just as there is not much difference between Buddha's nature and human nature. A major difference, though, exists between people who imitate Buddha's behavior and those who do not. The former are people willing to serve others, and who never succumb to the stressful spurs of difficulty. Also, they sacrifice their own interests if necessary.

"That is why they are not concerned about losses and gains. As for the latter ones, these people care unreasonably about what they gain and lose. We can say that the major difference between these two groups of people is whether they possess a religious man's conviction: that is, to live for the well-being of all living creatures."

A member asked about the importance of implementation in the process of imitating Buddha's behavior.

The Master said: "Buddha is a holy man with both good fortune and wisdom. If we want to have Buddha's good fortune and wisdom, we must cultivate them by performing practical acts as a way to implement our good intentions for helping all living creatures. As I often say, to become as good as Buddha is our goal as ordinary people. Being ordinary is the starting point for setting out toward that goal. But it is important to realize that the goal can only be realized by implementing the Bodhisattva moral: 'do good things for all living creatures.'"

A member asked: "We sometimes perform meritorious deeds on behalf of someone who is dead. What is the meaning of this?"

The Master answered: "You should sincerely want to do something for the dead. Both the doer and the dead will be blessed; the former will obtain reward for the meritorious deed, while the later will have contributed to the world by being a point of motivation for you to become a Buddhist."

T he Diamond Sutra says, one cannot hold on to the concepts of being and non-being. What does this mean?

The Master commented: "One should not hold on to these two concepts; one should adopt the rule of golden means. Upsetting the scales will make an imbalance. The philosophy of life is in fact very simple; we need only to perceive it through our daily conduct, such as when walking or eating. Even so, we must not cling to the philosophy of life in an extreme way; to do so could make it difficult to accomplish our work. A man will always behave properly if he can keep the philosophy of life and his practical work in balance. Thus, he will not be clinging to either the concept of being or of non-being."

A member asked: "What is the significance of Amitabha?"

The Master replied: "It stands for infinite age, light and wisdom. It, therefore, contains many good wishes."

A member asked: "Is the ceremony for feeding the ghosts, held on the 15th day of the 7th moon, a Buddhist or Taoist festival? Or, is it a folk religion festival? Also, is it against Buddha's philosophy to celebrate this festival in an extravagant way?"

The Master replied: "It is called the Ullambana Festival according to Buddhist doctrine. Ullambana is a Sanscrit word meaning 'to hang upside-down,' which refers to the extreme suffering of the ghosts of hunger in purgatory. The throats of the ghosts of hunger are as slim as needles; they cannot swallow any amount of food. We often offer sailing vessels, filled with food offerings, to the Buddhist trinity for the purpose of releasing from purgatory the souls of those who have died. This is the All Souls Festival. A good Buddhist should have a deep understanding of this festival. Do not waste your time and energy on meaningless, extravagant rituals. Otherwise, you will misunderstand the Buddhist doctrine and violate the anti-superstition and thrift programs promoted by our government."

---

member asked: "Why do Buddhists stress the importance of chanting Buddha's name for the benefit of people who are in a terminal stage?"

The Master answered: "When a person is dying, his nerves are on the brink of becoming inoperative. It is a painful moment in the life of the patient. We can help him feel less unhappy by chanting Buddha's name. Also, the sound of our voices will help the spirits concentrate in order to resist the temptation of evil ghosts."

---

student asked: "There are quite a few Bodhisattvas, but why do most people like to worship the Goddess of Mercy?"

270 The Master answered: "This is because the Goddess of

Mercy has a more intimate relationship with the living creatures. She has cultivated a strong capacity of comprehension, specializing in listening to the lamenting of living creatures. Although living creatures can endure their pain, they feel relieved when receiving the care and concern of someone merciful. This goddess is certainly merciful; that is why people feel close to her."

A Master's disciple asked: "How can I cultivate the ability of entrancement?"

The Master said: "Make mental concentration a habit. You can cultivate the ability of entrancement once you can fully concentrate your mind."

A commissioner of the Tzu Chi Foundation commented: "Physical fatigue does not bother me at all. But what I really recoil from is the friction between people I work with."

The Master replied: "If you want to follow in the Bodhisattvas' footsteps, you must not be afraid to face difficulties or challenges, whether physical or mental. You can only achieve the goal of becoming a good man like Buddha by enduring all the friction between people.

"Don't quit when you face problems. To Buddha, everyone is entitled to become an enlightened man such as he. What worries Buddha, is that we might yield to trouble on our way to enlightenment."

A secular Buddhist asked: "How can people like me eliminate our attachment to a particular cause or idea?"

The Master answered: "Any secular Buddhist who wants to cultivate virtue must first cultivate the tranquillity of his mind. If a secular Buddhist does not have a tranquil mind, he cannot finish his study of Buddha's philosophy. It would be difficult for you to eliminate worries if you were always thinking of your attachments."

A member asked: "It is so difficult to cultivate virtue. I have encountered a lot of setbacks. What should I do?"

The Master answered: "Try to perceive Buddha's philosophy thoroughly. However, you should not take the worldly human affairs too seriously. We work with ordinary people everyday; of course we will face disagreements. Though we might become upset by these things, we should learn to remain calm in our deepest heart. So, don't quit. Try as best you can to behave like the Bodhisattvas."

A member asked about the right way to repent.

The Master said: "Let bygones be bygones. Don't repeat the same sins in the future. Seize the day so you can accomplish as many good deeds as possible to perform your penance."

Speaking About Karmaic Hindrances

A member asked: "Why do we often hurt each other?"

The Master answered: "This can be attributed to the mental poisons of greed and anger. A man's anger is often spawned by his greed. When a man is angry, he tends to hurt others."

A member asked: "Some people cultivate themselves by the wrong practices. Why is that?"

The Master explained: "Often we see a man who appears to have acquired a lot of wisdom after cultivating himself with Buddhist practice, and yet still cannot eliminate all the attachments and worries in his heart. He is the type who has cultivated himself with the wrong practices."

A member asked: "What are Karmaic hindrances?"

The Master answered: "Sometimes a person prevents you from doing something you intended to do. He obstructs you because you did the same thing to him once before. The ill deed committed in the past created a bad Karma. This sort of preventive action is what we call a Karmaic hindrance."

After learning meditation and some meditative kung fu, a once shy and melancholy boy grew hungry for magical powers and often spoke of achieving immortality. The 10-year-old's concerned parents took the child to see the Master.

The Master said to him: "The illusions in your mind

are like the images on a TV screen. You see them when you switch on your mental TV. It would be better for an energetic young man like you to take part in more outdoor activities. Try to get closer to the natural environment. You can accumulate a lot of misconceptions if you lock yourself in a room playing magic games or meditating all day long. Only a healthy body can bring you a healthy life. You will live an empty life, if you only care about the things that do not exist. Do not heed every strange sound you think you hear, for doing so will surely make you nervous. Turn a deaf ear, and they will soon fade."

---

 member asked: "Someone said women have more Karmaic hindrances than do men. Is this correct?"

The Master answered: "Not necessarily. However, each woman learns to adjust herself in accordance with her Karma. Also, a woman's strength will become great if she is truly determined.

"Avalokitesvara Bodhisattva is a good example; he

often became transformed before the world into the feminine form of the Goddess of Mercy. How merciful a woman's heart can be! Mercy breeds wisdom, and you can then help promote the work of saving the world. A women should not underestimate herself."

(*Speaking About Converting*)

A member asked about the significance of converting to Buddhism.

The Master replied: "To do so means that a person forsakes darkness for light. Before he converts to Buddhism, his heart is filled with dark thoughts. After he converts, he progresses in the bright side of life, eliminating all his faults, acting with proper diligence and prudence, and resolutely and bravely carrying out the goodness, beauty and truth of life.

"As Buddha's disciples, we should be as merciful as Buddha.

"Though we might have once been rude to another, even throwing things when feeling offended, we should now correct all such mistakes. Try to treat others with an accommodating and loving heart. The significance of converting lies not in obtaining Buddha's blessings, but in cultivating a heart that is full of love and sincerity."

Appendix

1 The following is translated from an article

By Lin Chin-hsun, as appearing in the Jan. 7, 1990 issue of the Chinese-language Min Sheng Daily News :

The publication of Master Cheng Yen's *Still Thoughts, Volume One* is indeed a delightful event. We can hardly find a book as pure and clean as this one on Taiwan's book market today.

Master Cheng Yen has donated all the proceeds from her book to the Tzu Chi Association. Kao Hsing-chiang volunteered his expertise as managing editor of the book project, and the Chiou Ko Publishing Co. is selling the book at an extremely low price in order to promote its circulation.

In money-oriented societies such as Taiwan, the publication of a book such as *Still Thoughts*, with its many touching stories, has the potential to easily inspire people.

Since 1988 Kao Hsing-chiang, a distinguished figure in the fields of mass media, publishing and cultural activities, was deeply moved by Master Cheng Yen's great spirit of mercy two years ago. Kao left his work of over 20 years to join the Tzu Chi Association, which made headline news.

After joining Tzu Chi, his first meritorious deed was to make the association the subject of reports so that Master Cheng Yen's benevolence could become better known to the general public. His second contribution was to compile and edit the original Chinese version of Master Cheng Yen's *Still Thoughts*.

Unlike solemn Buddhist publications, *Still Thoughts* welcomes the reader with an accessible, lively and vivid style. It transcends ordinary publications by opening up new possibilities with its "quotations" style. Kao's detailed editing work makes the book a first-class publication.

Obviously, though, the real significance regarding the publication of the book is how it illustrates Master Cheng Yen's genuine personality, or in other words how it presents us with her explanatory notes on wisdom and mercy. The book also provides insight to Master Cheng Yen's first-hand experiences, and how she implemented Buddha's philosophy through her depiction of the spiritual careers of the Tzu Chi Association.

Expanding the book into a series would surely have a positive impact on correcting social ills in Taiwan. We eagerly await experiencing more profound and touching guidance in the second volume of Master Cheng Yen's *Still Thoughts*.

2 The following is translated from Lee Rei-tung's article titled "Harmonious Wisdom and Merciful Feeling," as appearing in the Dec. 2, 1989, issue of the Chinese-language United Daily News

The "quotations" style is a traditional literary form in China. The speakers were often saints or great philosophers, and their words were recorded by their disciples or students. Examples can be found in the "Confucian Analects," The Quotations of Scholars in the Song and Ming Dynasties, and Chang Tai-yen's Sublime Discourses From Ching-han.

Generally speaking, books of this style are often concise and simple. They do not have many elaborations, yet are full of wisdom.

STILL THOUGHTS

Master Cheng Yen's *Still Thoughts* can be viewed as another good example of the style. This book clearly demonstrates an enlightened Buddhist nun's harmonious wisdom, and her merciful feeling toward all living creatures.

Master Cheng Yen spreads her blessings and good wishes throughout the turbulent human world. She talks about our daily matters with simple, but wise words, helping us in terms of our virtue-cultivation.

The book was edited by Kao Hsing-chiang, one of the most prominent editors in Taiwan. ... The words in the book are simple, but the meanings are profound. Keep the book around, so that it can be studied and put into practice.

3 The following is from Lee Chin's article Good Advice That Does Not Sound Unpleasant as appearing in the Dec. 2, 1989, issue of the United Daily News. The writer is a Chinese pianist livingin the United States

In September 1989, I came to Taiwan at the invitation of the New Aspect Cultural Promotion Center to take part in cultural exchange programs.

Prior to my return to the U.S., my friends Mr. and Mrs. Ho gave me a copy of Master Cheng Yen's *Still Thoughts*. Also, they asked me to forward another two copies to the renowned musicians Ma Yo-yo and Lin Cho-liang.

Still Thoughts has become my intimate source for cheering me up when I feel frustrated, and for keeping me humble and calm when I feel triumphant. Each word in the

STILL THOUGHTS

book speaks nothing but the truth. To me, it is good advice that does not sound unpleasant.

4 *The following was written by Chang Ai-chuan*

Good luck, good health and less burden are the hopes we ordinary people dream to have. However, only a few people really consider what they should do if things do not turn out the way they wish, when suffering from bad health or when their big burdens never lessen.

Escapism is often the temporary solution for avoiding our troubles, but in the long run problems resurface. The future will only become bright after we bravely face and solve our problems.

Our bodies are too mysterious to understand, and the life cycle of birth, aging, illness and death is unavoidable. People's minds turn pessimistic and low-spirited when the body is in poor health. But an ill man will remain wise and loving when he has a resolute and determined heart.

Consider the Taiwan singer Hsuh Yueh. He was very ill. Yet, before dying he made a series of public service advertisements encouraging everyone in society to cherish the value of life. He showed his care and concern for society.

This summer, I had to bear great burdens and pressures generated by my work, family and relatives. I felt frustrated and tired, both physically and mentally. All I wished for was to run off to a remote area, so that I could be left alone. But suddenly an inspiring idea flashed across my mind: "Give it a shot!" I said to myself. I resolved to see just how much I could accomplish. And just like that I began finishing one task after another. I feel good now.

When I made a wish in the past, I often asked for peace, health and happiness. Today is New Year's Day 1991. After reading the essay, Three New Wishes in the New Spring, set down in Master Cheng Yen's *Still Thoughts,* I have a new, sort of mixed feeling in my heart. I feel ashamed of myself for being so childish and cowardly before. However, at the same time, I feel happy to have found a new goal in life.

It is true that 90 percent of our wishes do not turn out the way we expected. But we will fear nothing, when we are brave enough to face reality. The life cycle of birth, aging, illness and death is beyond our control. However, we can help people as much as possible when we have wisdom and love. It is impossible for us to avoid our burdens. We can shoulder those burdens, though, when we have strength and capability.

I am happy today after reading "Three New Wishes in the New Spring" which to me are like an infallible law. I have changed my ideas and views in life. I am willing to share this happiness with all of you.

(on New Year's Day 1991)

5 *The following was written*
By Lee Li-or

For a long time since my late-husband was first hospitalized, my heart was not able to remain calm. Life for me was filled with annoyances and fears. I had a hard time distinguishing between the things that happened before and things that were happening at the present. I dared not imagine how I would live in the future. Though I knew it was not best, I could not refrain from submerging myself in memories.

It might seem hard to believe that a woman born in a Buddhist family would fail to mold her character appropriately via the influence of Buddhism. But, in fact, I apparently knew nothing about such Buddhist concepts as Karma

292

or life being filled with changes.

During the period of painful days, Master Yin Cheng, my second elder sister who became a Buddhist nun, tried her best to console me by telling me the true meaning of Karma, and by taking me to various places to study Buddha's philosophy. My concept of life remained pessimistic and my grievous mental wounds stayed unhealed, even though I received instruction from a few Buddhist masters.

Master Yin Cheng recently became acquainted with Chuan Chih, who worked in the Tzu Chi Association's Tai-chung office. Chuan Chih encouraged me to join Tzu Chi, and also gave me a copy of Still Thoughts. After carefully reading the book twice, I realized how wrong I had been.

Try to perceive the true essence of life with wisdom, and arrange the time in your life with resolution, Master Cheng Yen says in her book. I was completely awakened by this sentence. After giving it a closer reading the second time, I refused to be attached any longer to the annoyances and unhappy incidents that were making my life miserable and my children's lives joyless.

STILL THOUGHTS

This happened to me some time ago. Since then I have been gradually changing my attitude toward life. Though I cannot fully relax as yet due to the severity of strain I went through for so long, I have resolved to imitate Buddha's behavior. I intend to offer my love to all living creatures, and to do many meaningful things.

BUDDHIST COMPASSION RELIEF TZU-CHI FOUNDATION

◉HEAD ASSOCIATION:21, KANG LEH VILLAGE, SHIN CHERNG SHIANG, HUALIEN TAIWAN, R.O.C.

TEL:(038)266779 FAX:(038)26776

◉TAIPEI BRANCH & BUDDHIST TZU-CHI CULTURAL CENTER:35, ALLEY 7, LANE 217, SEC 3, CHUNG HSIAO E.RD., TAIPEI, TAIWAN R.O.C

TEL:(02)7760111 FAX:(02)77660615

◉TAI CHUNG BRANCH:2, LANE 314, MIN CHUAN RD., TAI CHUNG, TAIWAN, R.O.C.

TEL:(04)3224073 FAX:(04)3229616

◉KAOHSIUNG BRANCH OFFICE:3 F, NO. 150, JYOU RU SECOND RD. KAOHSIUNG, TAIWAN, R.O.C

◉PING DONG BRANCH:83－1 JONG SHING RD., CHARNG SHING VILLAGE, CHARNG CHIH SHIANG, PING DONG, TAIWAN, R.O.C.

TEL:(08)7363953 FAX:(08)7366853

◉TZU－CHI BUDDHIST GENERAL HOSPITAL:8 SHIN－SHENG S.RD., HUALIEN, TAIWAN, R.O.C.

TEL:(038)561825 FAX:(038)560977

◉TZU－CHI JR. COLLEGE OF NURSING:143－100 DER SHING RD., HUALIEN, TAIWAN, R.O.C.

TEL:(038)572158～9 FAX:(038)577261

◉BUDDHSIT COMPASSION RELIEF TZU－CHI FOUNDATION U.S.A.: 1000 SOUTH GARFLELD AVE., ALHAMBRA, CALIE 91801 U.S.A.

TEL:(818)305－1188 FAX:(818)3051185

◉BUDDHIST COMPASSION RELIEF TZU－CHI FOUNDATION U.S.A., TEXAS OFFICE 6515 CORPORATE DRIVE, SUITE R, HOUSTON, TEXAS 77036 U.S.A.

TEL:(713)9818960 FAX:(713)9819008

◉BUDDHIST COMPASSION RELIEF TZU－CHI FOUNDATION U.S.A.,

NEW YORK BRANCH:36–09 MAIN ST, ROOM 10B, FLUSHING, NEW YORK 11354 U.S.A.

TEL:(718)4604590 FAX:(718)4602068

◉CANADA LIAISON OFFICE: TEL:1–604–2443166. FAX:1–604–2447962.

◉BRAZIL LIAISON OFFICE: TEL:55–11–2770468. FAX:55–11–2710706.

◉ARGENTINA LIAISON OFFICE: TEL & FAX:541–7847233.

◉GREAT BRITAIN LIAISON OFFICE: TEL:44–81–5607729. FAX:44–81–5687761

◉SOUTH AFRICA LIAISON OFFICE: TEL:27–11–8499953. FAX:27–11–4251790.

◉AUSTRALIA LIAISON OFFICE: TEL:61–7–3456124. FAX:61–7–3454867

◉HONG KONG LIAISON OFFICE: TEL:852–8937106. FAX:852–8937478.

◉SINGAPORE LIAISON OFFICE: TEL:65–2561725. FAX:65–2518376

◉MALAYSIA LIAISON OFFICE: TEL & FAX:604–2286561

◉ BUDDHIST COMPASSION RELIEF (TZU–CHI) FOUNDATION, JAPAN BRANCH: ROOM:901 CO–OP TOWA WAKABAYASHI, TOKYO, 154, JAPAN.

TEL:(81)3–34130439 FAX:(81)3–34130789

佛教慈濟美國文化出版中心
**BUDDHIST TZU CHI CULTURE
& PUBLISHING CENTER, USA**
4031 Peck Rd., El Monte, CA 91732
Tel:818-579-5557 • Fax:818-579-1308